Home Coffee Roasting

Also by Kenneth Davids

Coffee: A Guide to Buying, Brewing & Enjoying

Espresso: Ultimate Coffee

Home Coffee Roasting

ROMANCE & REVIVAL

KENNETH DAVIDS

St. Martin's Griffin
New York

Drawings and maps copyright © 1996 by Ginny Pruitt and Kenneth Davids except as follows:

Courtesy of *Tea & Coffee Trade Journal.* Display ornament. Drawings on pages 3, 19, 25, 27, 28, 34, 39 (bottom), 43 (bottom), 44 (top), 44 (bottom), 45, 48 (top), 48 (bottom), 49 (top), 71, 72, 75, 86.

Courtesy of Idealibri, an imprint of Rusconi Libri, Milan. Drawing on page 5.

Courtesy of Kevin Sinnott. Drawings on pages 26, 104.

Courtesy of David M. Cochran. Drawing on page 42.

Courtesy of Harold Gell and Brian Porto. Drawing on page 41 (bottom).

The roast color tiles reproduced on the inside back cover appear courtesy of the Specialty Coffee Association of America and its Executive Director, Ted Lingle.

The long passage from Eduardo De Filippo in Chapter 1 appears courtesy of Idealibri, an imprint of Rusconi Libri, Milan. Reprinted by permission.

Design by Deborah Daly

LIBRARY OF CONGRESS CATALOGING-IN-PUBLICATION DATA

Davids, Kenneth.
    Home coffee roasting : romance & revival / by Kenneth Davids.—1st ed.
        p.   cm.
    ISBN 0-312-14111-4
    1. Coffee. 2. Coffee—Processing. 3. Coffee brewing. I. Title.
TX415.D43   1996
641.3'373—dc20   95-33722
                                                              CIP

First St. Martin's Griffin Edition: May 1996

10 9 8 7 6 5 4 3 2 1

ACKNOWLEDGMENTS

The generosity of people in the specialty coffee business may have been tested by this project. I suspect that many harbored doubts concerning the viability of home roasting. Nevertheless, all assisted me with their usual grace, passion, and intelligence.

Jim Reynolds of Peet's Coffee & Tea and Warren Muller, formerly of Peerless and now of Cargill Coffee, were constantly, often almost daily, liberal with information and opinion, not to mention green coffees. My newsletter-writing colleague Kevin Sinnott provided a soundingboard, ideas, and a nonstop flow of phone numbers and contacts garnered by his indefatigable networking. Carl Staub's roasting seminar at Agtron and the work of Michael Sivetz supplied much of the technical information incorporated here. Michael Glenister of Amcafe generously shared his detailed knowledge of African and Pacific coffees, shedding light on questions that have puzzled me since I wrote my first coffee book twenty years ago. As for the dozens of others who contributed to this book (often without realizing it), I can only list a few: Cynthia Barbe and Melissa Iserloth of Kaanapali Coffee; Ian Bersten, coffee writer and manufacturer of the Roller Roaster; Angela Caruso of Berardi's Fresh Roast; David Cochran of Mac-Cochran Coffee; Dan Cox of Coffee Enterprises; David Dallis of Dallis Brothers; Steve Diedrich of Diedrich Coffee Roasters; Sherman Dodd of Coffee/PER; Jay Endres of Roastery Development Group; Frank and Joan Elevitch of Palani Plantation; Bill Felknor of Felknor International; Jamie Fortuño of Yauco Selecto; inventor Harold Gell; Michael Glenister of Amcafe; Joseph John of Josuma Coffee; Paul Kalenian of Armeno Coffee Roasters; Erna Knutsen and John Rapinchuk of Knutsen Coffees; Ted Lingle, Executive Director of the Specialty Coffee Association of America; Mohamed Moledina of Moledina Commodities; John Nicolet of Rair Systems; Robert Piacente of Island Coffee, Tea & Spice; entrepreneur Steven Pitock; Rick Ray of Melchers Flavors of America; Roger Sandon, publisher of *Café Olé* magazine; Don Schoenholt of Gillies Coffee; T. J. Tjokroadisumarto of the Association of Indonesian Coffee Exporters; and George Vukasin of Peerless Coffee. There were many, many others; were I to continue I would end by listing a quarter of the membership of the Specialty Coffee Association of America.

As usual I cluttered up many a café table during the writing of this book. The tables in Coffee Head of Oakland, California, were particularly congenial.

Moving from coffee to publishing I wish to thank my illustrator Ginny Pruitt; *Tea & Coffee Trade Journal* for its very generous permission to reproduce illustrations from William Ukers's *All About Coffee*; Rusconi Libri of Milan for permission to quote Eduardo De Filippo and reprint his drawing; and Kevin Sinnott, once again, for use of illustrations from his collection. The enthusiastic support of my agent, Richard Derus of Claudia Menza Literary Agency, and my editor, Keith Kahla of St. Martin's Press, is deeply appreciated.

All of these people (and café tables) deserve any credit due this book, whereas the mistakes and defects are entirely mine.

CONTENTS

5

Getting Started

Why Home Roasting?

Authenticity, Economy, Alchemy

A few minutes ago I roasted several days' supply of coffee in a stove-top popcorn popper. The whole process took about ten minutes. The popper can be purchased in any well-stocked housewares department for $20 to $25. The coffee I roasted (a fancy Sumatra) might cost (at the moment's somewhat inflated prices) anywhere from $5 to $6 a pound green, or less if I bought it wholesale. The same coffee purchased roasted at the corner coffee store would cost $8 to $10 a pound. The coffee I produced was fresher than almost any I could have bought, and its freshness by far compensated for any small failings in roasting procedure. Green coffee beans keep well without special handling, so the modest effort required to purchase them (through the mail or by special arrangement with a retailer or wholesaler) doesn't need to be undertaken often.

Nor was the stove-top popper my only option. I could have chosen to roast the coffee in a gas oven, for example, or in one of a certain design of hot-air corn popper, or in a device specially designed for home roasting.

Given its simplicity—once you know what you're doing, basic home coffee roasting ranks in difficulty somewhere between boiling an egg and making a good white sauce—why don't more people do it? Why isn't home coffee roasting already as popular as home baking, for example, or home pasta making, or—for that matter—home corn popping?

First, most people simply don't know how vibrant truly fresh coffee tastes when compared to the partly staled version we usually drink. Almost everyone knows how exquisite fresh bread is, or how much better home-popped popcorn is than the chewy, rubbery stuff that comes in bags. But the fragrance of coffee one day out of the roaster is a virtually forgotten pleasure.

1

Second, people don't know that roasting coffee at home is easy and fun, and something that everyone did before the victory of advertising and convenience foods.

Lettuce Comes from the Store

I once worked as a counselor in a day camp. One day while on a nature hike I invited the children to take bites of an edible weed Californians call miner's lettuce. Several refused, on the basis that the leaves came out of the dirt and bugs had crawled on them. When I pointed out that they all ate lettuce, and that lettuce also came out of the dirt and risked having bugs crawl on it, one child objected. "Lettuce doesn't come from the dirt," she declared. "Lettuce comes from the store!"

By mid-twentieth century Americans thought of "coffee" as granulated brown stuff that came from a can rather than the dried seeds of a tree requiring only a few relatively simple procedures to transform it into a beverage. As happened in the twentieth century with so many other foods and manufacturers, the actual facts about coffee's origin (it consists of vegetable matter that has been dried, roasted, and ground by human beings) were replaced by market-driven substitute facts (coffee is brown granules produced by the complex machinery of an all-knowing corporation).

Of course, at the very moment of victory for brand-name convenience foods (say about 1960), a countermovement set in wherein the individuals who had recently come to be called consumers began turning themselves back into cooks or wine-makers or brewers or bakers. In the world of coffee the return to more authentic foods took the form of the specialty-coffee movement, which advocated a revival of the nineteenth-century practice of selling freshly roasted coffee beans in bulk, and encouraged coffee lovers to take their beans home and grind them themselves. It is unusual in America today to find anyone interested in eating and drinking well who doesn't buy coffee in bulk as whole beans and grind the beans themselves before brewing.

There is no doubt that whole-bean coffees handled well are a tremendous advance in flavor and variety over supermarket packaged blends, and certainly anyone not yet introduced to the adventure of fine coffee should start by simply buying whole-bean coffee at the local specialty coffee store, learning to grind and brew it properly, and experiencing some of the variety and pleasures it affords.

However, for the committed coffee aficionado, home coffee roasting is a logical next step toward closer intimacy with the bean and a mastery of one's own pleasure.

Nostalgia, Balconies, and Roasting Smoke

Throughout most of coffee history people roasted their own beans. Even in the United States, the cradle of convenience, preroasted coffee did not catch on until the latter years of the nineteenth century. Home roasting persisted in Mediterranean countries like Italy until well after World War II, and many coffee drinkers in the Middle East and the horn of Africa still roast their own coffee as part of a leisurely ritual combining roasting, brewing, and drinking in one long sitting.

Museum collections are full of wonderful old home coffee-roasting devices. One of the options you could buy with your fashionable new wood stove in nineteenth-century America was a home coffee roaster, usually in the form of a hollow cast-iron globe that fit inside one of the burner openings.

For people in countries where home roasting was the norm through the first half of the twentieth century, the practice is rich with nostalgia. Listen to Eduardo De Filippo, for example, a well-known Italian writer and performer, recollecting coffee roasting in his childhood Naples in Mariarosa Schiaffino's *Le Ore del Caffè*:

An elaborate Italian home roaster from the seventeenth century. It probably doubled as a heat stove. A charcoal fire burned inside the double doors at the bottom of the device. When someone—doubtless a servant—wanted to roast coffee, the top lid with its elaborate tulip sculpture would be removed and replaced by the round roasting chamber with crank pictured on the floor in front.

In 1908 ... in the streets and alleys of Naples, in the first hours of the morning, a very special ritual was celebrated, a ritual indispensable to less wealthy families as well as to better-off aficionados: the ceremony of coffee roasting. It saved money to buy raw coffee beans and then roast them at home, the only cost being personal skillfulness and patience. Every week (or every couple of weeks) a quantity of coffee was roasted, depending on the needs, finances, and appetites of each family.

And since these rituals were not simultaneous, every day somewhere in the neighborhood a woman or grandpa could be found sitting on the family balcony, turning the crank of the *abbrustulaturo,* or coffee roaster.

We now need to describe this object, today only a memory for most Neapolitans. It was a metal cylinder of thirty to sixty centimeters in length, with a diameter of about fifteen [twelve to twenty-four inches by six inches]. Protruding from one end of the cylinder was a long pin; from the other a crank. Raw coffee beans were placed inside the cylinder through a small door in its side, which was firmly held closed by a little hook. The lower part of the device consisted of a rectangular steel box; inside the box a small charcoal fire was lit. At the top of either end of the box were grooves into which the pin and the crank fit, supporting the cylinder between them over the fire. Once the cylinder was placed atop the box the roasting could begin.

By the way: Why did I mention balconies? Because in the process of such roasting the coffee beans, which are quite oily, release an intense smoke that could be quite unbearable in a closed space, yet no nuisance at all out-of-doors. Instead, dispersed in the air and transported by the wind, it was a source of great happiness for the entire neighborhood.

As the crank was turned the beans tossed up and down against the hot cylinder wall until they were roasted just right. Occasionally the cylinder had to be taken off the base and shaken a few times to check the sound the beans made, so as to judge their weight, since they became lighter as they roasted. But that was not enough ... the color of the beans had to be checked through the small door in the side of the cylinder, and when they were the "color of a monk's tunic," as we said, the cylinder was quickly removed from the fire and the roasted beans poured onto a large tray or terra-cotta plate. There they were carefully stirred with a wooden ladle until they cooled. With every stroke the roasting smoke would permeate the air with a delicious, intense, irresistible aroma.

As for me—lingering about in bed during those early hours, trying to delay the moment when I would have to get up and go to school—as soon as this seductive smell reached my nose (it even penetrated the closed windows!) I would jump out of bed full of energy, happy to begin the day. And so it was that, even before I was allowed to drink it, coffee became my wake-up call and symbol for the new day....

This freshly-roasted coffee fragrance, one of the finest of aromas, would follow me as I washed myself, as I dressed, as I devoured my "'a zupp' e latte" or milk soup, and as I descended the stairs.... Down in the street the smell wouldn't be as strong ... but I still would be made aware of it by the voices I heard. The comments crackled from window to window along my way from home to school. "Ah, what fragrance, what pleasure!" street vendors might shout.

One skinny old woman might ask another with a bun of black hair: "Have you roasted your coffee yet?" And the other would reply: "Of course! We roast it twice a week. Grandpa is so picky he has to do it himself." On the balcony of an elegant apartment a servant, who looked like a wasp with his black-yellow striped jacket and black greased whiskers, to an exquisite maid in the apartment next door: "I'll have to leave you shortly: the coffee must be removed." And she would reply: "Yes, of course.... I roast it every Saturday; it is always a great responsibility, Ciro my dear...."

Also, quite often, just before being swallowed up by the school gate, my ear would intercept an "Ahhhh ...!" from a shoemaker nearby. Sipping his cup of coffee before starting work, his "Ahhhh ...!" was so expressive—you could feel pleasure, satisfaction, happiness, appetite, even surprise and wonder. Later, as an adult, I would discover all of those things in coffee myself. *

Some Reasons to Roast

For those of us who weren't raised with the scent of roasting coffee filling the narrow streets and picturesque balconies of memory, and whose childhood recollections instead involve tract homes, Pepsi-Cola, and Maxwell House, what are the advantages of home roasting? It may be a simple but forgotten art, yet why bother at all?

Eduardo De Filippo's drawing of the Neapolitan *abbrustulaturo,* or home coffee roaster, he describes on pages 3-4.

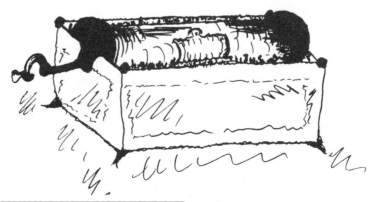

* Eduardo De Filippo, "Introduzione, *L'abbrustulaturo*," Mariarosa Schiaffino, *Le Ore del Caffè* (Milan: Idealibri, 1983), pp. 6–8. This translation by Emanuela Aureli and Kenneth Davids.

Here are a few reasons.

Freshness and flavor. Unlike stale bread, which rapidly becomes dramatically inedible, stale coffee still can be drunk and enjoyed. But what a difference a few days make! An absolutely fresh coffee, a day or two out of the roaster, explodes with perfume, an evanescent aroma that seems to resonate in the nervous system and vibrate around the head like a sort of coffee aura. The aftertaste of a truly fresh coffee can ring on the palate for an entire morning; the taste of a week-old coffee will vanish in a few minutes. Perhaps the persistent surprise and delight of De Filippo's shoemaker at the revelation of his morning coffee was partly owing to the fact that he had a grandpa who roasted it every week on the family balcony rather than buying it half stale at a supermarket.

Coffee is best about a day after it has been roasted. Once past that moment a rapid and relentless deterioration in flavor sets in as the protective envelope of carbon dioxide gas dissipates, allowing oxygen to penetrate the bean and stale the delicate flavor oils. For someone who genuinely loves coffee, the bouquet of optimally fresh beans is without doubt the most tangible of the many reasons to roast coffee at home.

Reasonably fresh coffee can be gotten at specialty stores if the roasting is done on the premises or close by, but with the growth of mammoth regional and national specialty-coffee chains beans may be roasted hundreds or even thousands of miles from the store where you finally buy them. Coffee from these specialty chains will be infinitely better and fresher than the preground stuff that comes in cans and bricks, but it won't—can't—be as fresh as the coffee you roast in your own kitchen.

Personal satisfaction. Roasting coffee at home provides the gratification many of us derive from outflanking consumerism by gaining control of a heretofore mysterious process that was once imposed on us by others. Home roasting is also an art—a minor one perhaps, but an art nonetheless, and one that can provide considerable gratification.

Money. Obviously this issue is more important to some than to others. Depending on how and where you buy your green coffee, you can save anywhere from 25 to 50 percent of the cost per pound by roasting at home. See Resources for strategies on finding sources for green coffee.

Connoisseurship. The way to truly understand a coffee is to roast it. Furthermore, home roasting makes it possible to develop what amounts to a cellar of green coffees. Unroasted coffee doesn't quite last indefinitely, but for a year or two it registers only subtle changes in flavor, and remains interesting and drinkable for years after that. Handled properly, some coffees even improve with age. Thus you can keep modest supplies of your favorite coffees around and select them for roasting according to your mood and your guests' inclinations. The coffee-cellar idea is discussed in more detail on pages 104–106.

Bragging rights. So there you are, roasting a blend of Guatemalan Huehuetenango and Sumatran Lintong, your kitchen pungent with smelly yet glamorous smoke, when your friends arrive for dinner carrying that pathetic bag of week-old house blend from down the street....

I won't add more because I don't want to encourage snobbery or one-upmanship, but you get the picture.

Romance. Finally, roasting your own coffee carries you deeper into the drama and romance of coffee, which I remain a sucker for despite twenty years of professional and semiprofessional involvement with the stuff. That romance is nowhere as vividly encapsulated as in that moment when a pile of hard, almost odorless gray-green seeds is suddenly and magically transformed into the fragrant vehicle of our dreams, reveries, and conversation. To be the magicians waving the wand of transformation makes that metamorphosis all the more stirring and resonant.

If You Can Read You Can Roast

And above all: *you can do it.* You couldn't get a job as a professional coffee roaster because professional roasters need to achieve precision and consistency as well as quality.

But anyone who can read this book can produce a decent to stunningly superb roast at home. Jabez Burns, probably the single greatest roasting innovator in American history, once said that some of the best coffee he had ever tasted was done in a home corn popper.

Liberating the Taste Genie

Chemistry and Drama of the Roast

What Happens to Coffee When It's Roasted?

In fact, no one knows—exactly. One of the many intriguing characteristics of coffee is the complexity of its aromatic agents—at this writing, 700 to 850 substances have been identified as possible contributors to the flavor of roasted coffee. The exact number of contributing substances varies from study to study and sample to sample, perhaps influenced by the geographical origin of the beans and how they are dried and prepared for market.

These figures do not include all of coffee's many additional non-flavor-influencing components. Over 2,000 substances have been identified in green arabica coffee beans.

These formidable numbers make coffee one of the most complex of commonly consumed foods and beverages. Wine, for example, has considerably fewer flavor-influencing constituents than coffee. Only about 150 components contribute to the taste of vanilla, considered by food chemists one of the more complicated of natural flavorings. To this day, the actual coffee part of "coffee-flavored" candies and other foods is derived from roasted coffee itself and not whipped up in a laboratory, a tribute to coffee's defiant complexity.

One thing is certain: the 700 to 850 flavor constituents of arabica coffee and their heady fragrance would not be available to us without roasting. Roasting is the act that liberates the taste genie of green coffee.

Very broadly, roasting (1) forces water out of the bean; (2) dries out and expands its woody parts, making them more porous and reducing the total weight of the bean by 14 to 20 percent; (3) sets off a continuous transformation of some sugars into CO^2 gas, a process that continues after the coffee is roasted and only concludes when the

8

coffee is definitively stale; (4) drives off some volatile substances, including a small part of the caffeine; and finally and most importantly, (5) caramelizes a portion of the bean's sugars and transforms some into what are popularly called the coffee's flavor oils: the tiny, fragile, yet potent mix of appetizing substances with unappetizing names like aldehydes, ketones, esters, and acetic, butyric, and valeric acids. It is the caramelized sugars, the flavor oils, and traces of other substances, like bitter trigonelline and quinic and nicotinic acids, that (along with the approximately 1 percent caffeine) give coffee drinkers the experience they pick up the cup for.

After roasting, the bean is in part reduced to a protective package for the caramelized sugars and flavor oils, which are secreted in tiny pockets throughout the bean's now woody, porous interior (or, in dark roasts, partly forced to the surface of the bean, giving these roasts their characteristic oily appearance). The carbon dioxide gas gradually works its way out of the bean in a process called degassing, which temporarily protects the flavor oils from the penetration of oxygen and staling. (Of course, when the CO_2 is finally gone, so is flavor. Vacuum cans, nitrogen-flushed bags, and so on are all artificial efforts to protect the coffee from the staling penetration of oxygen. And when the natural protective package formed by the bean is destroyed by grinding, the protective gas disappears even more quickly.)

The Drama of the Roast

If that's what happens inside the bean during roasting, what happens on the outside?

For the first few minutes after being introduced into the heat of the roasting chamber, nothing much. The beans remain grayish-green and mute, then they begin to yellow and emit a grassy or burlap-like odor. Next comes a steam that smells vaguely like bread or grain.

Finally, anywhere from two to fifteen minutes into the roasting cycle (depending on the volume of beans being roasted and the intensity of the heat in the roasting chamber), the steam darkens slightly in color and begins to smell like coffee. Then the first popping or crackling sounds make themselves heard.

This first crack, as coffee people call it, signals the definite start of the roast transformation or pyrolysis. Inside the bean sugars begin to caramelize; water bound up in the structure of the bean begins to split off from carbon dioxide, causing the series of tiny internal cata-

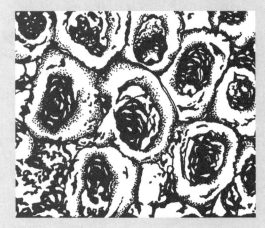

clysms that provoke the crackling sound. The still moist, now increasingly oily roasting smoke continues to rise from the beans.

The drawing on the left depicts a magnification of a cross-section of a green coffee bean; the drawing on the right a similar section of a roasted bean. Note the irregular, rumpled forms and solid structure of the green bean, and the hollow, open cells (often harboring droplets of volatile flavor oils) of the roasted bean.

From this point forward the beans begin to produce their own inner heat, precise and measurable, rising from around 350°F/175°C at the beginning of pyrolysis to about 435°F/225°C for a medium roast, to as high as 475°F/245°C in a very dark roast.

The beans darken in color as the roast progresses, an effect mainly caused by the caramelization of sugars and secondarily by the transformation of certain acids. The roast may be terminated at any time after pyrolysis begins, from early on when the beans are a very light brown in color, to late in the drama when they reach a very dark-brown, almost black color. The odor of the roasting smoke also subtly changes, reflecting (to experienced nostrils) the evolving roast style of the beans.

As the beans reach the middle ranges of brown the first wave of relatively subdued crackling gradually diminishes. Then, in roasts carried to a darker style, a second, more powerful wave of crackling sets in (the second crack), probably caused by the breakdown of the woody structures of the bean as still more substances volatilize. As this second round of crackling grows in intensity, so does the roasting smoke—now become dark, pungent, and even more abundant.

The progress of the roast can be measured in three ways: by the odor of the smoke (this was the favored approach to controlling the roast in the nineteenth century), by the inner temperature of the bean (the preferred approach of today's more technically inclined roasters), or by the surface color of the bean, color that can be read either by an experienced eye or by a sophisticated machine. The visual inspection of color is probably the most widely practiced method today, and the one most easily adopted by home roasters. Monitoring the roast by bean temperature dominates large-scale commercial roasting and is increasingly practiced by small-scale professional roasters as well, while controlling the roast through the changing fragrance of the roasting smoke is an almost lost art, carried on by only a handful of roasters trained in small shops during the earlier years of the twentieth century.

The same coffee bean brought to the same color or degree of roast by two different roasters will taste *roughly* similar; in other words, the *taste contributed by the roast* will be analogous if not identical. Differences in flavor among similar beans brought to the same degree of roast by different roasters are the result of variations in roasting equipment, method, and philosophy.

Some roasters prefer to develop a coffee slowly by subjecting it to relatively low temperatures in the roast chamber; others prefer a faster roast at higher temperatures. Still others vary the temperature as the roast progresses, raising the temperature in various increments at the moment the free moisture is eliminated from the bean and pyrolysis begins. These differences in method, a matter of pride and intense conviction on the part of individual coffee roasters, contribute to the richness and diversity of the world of fine coffee.

From Spoon to Fluid Beds

Roasting History

The discovery that the seeds of the coffee fruit tasted good when roasted was undoubtedly the key moment in coffee history. It marked the beginning of the transformation of coffee from an obscure medicinal herb known only in the horn of Africa and southern Arabia to the most popular beverage in the world, a beverage so widely drunk that today its trade generates more money than any other commodity except oil.

A skeptic might counter that it is caffeine, not flavor (or the roasting necessary to develop that flavor), that made coffee into one of the world's most important commodities. This argument is difficult to sustain, however. Tea, yerba maté, cocoa, coca, and other less famous plants also contain substances that wake us up and make us feel good. Yet none has achieved quite the same universal success as coffee.

Furthermore coffee—coffee *without* the caffeine—figures as an important flavoring in countless candies, cakes, and confections. And people sensitive to caffeine happily choose to drink decaffeinated coffee in preference to other caffeine-free beverages.

So clearly the aromatics of roasted coffee have a great deal to do with its triumph. On the other hand, there is evidence that the taste of coffee takes some getting used to. Children do not spontaneously like coffee, for example. And from coffee's first appearances in human culture to the present people have tended to add things to it. The first recorded coffee drinkers enhanced the beverage with cardamom and other spices, a tendency that continues today with flavored coffees and espresso drinks augmented with syrups, garnishes, and milk.

More than likely it is *both* the aromatic characteristics of roasted coffee and its stimulant properties that hooked humanity. At some point people began to associate the stimulating effect of coffee with the dark resonance of its taste, and further combined those associations with the myriad social satisfactions that began to cluster around the beverage: coming to consciousness in the morning, hospitality, conversation, the reveries of cafés. Thus the entire package—stimulation, taste, and social ritual—came together to mean *coffee* in all of its complexity and richness.

Coffee-Leaf Tea and Coffee-Fruit Frappés

We can only speculate how coffee was consumed before the advent of roasting sometime in the sixteenth century. However, the practices of some African societies in the regions where the coffee tree grows wild give us clues.

Ethiopian tribal peoples make tea from the leaves of the coffee tree, for example. Other recorded customs include chewing the dried fruit, pressing it into cakes, infusing it, mashing the ripe coffee fruit into a drink, and eating the crushed seeds imbedded in animal fat.

It is difficult to believe that coffee would have become the beverage of choice of most of the world if the only way to experience it was by infusing its leaves, putting its rather meager, thin-pulped fruit in a blender, or chewing on its raw seeds. Furthermore, there is at least some evidence that coffee's accelerated success over the past two centuries may be in part owing to continuous improvements in the understanding and technology of roasting, which, inference suggests, have produced an increasingly attractive beverage.

Mysterious Origins

Who first thought of roasting the seeds of the coffee tree and why?

We will doubtless never know. The early history of coffee in human culture is as obscure as the origin of most of the world's great foods. All that is known is based on inferences drawn from a few scattered references in written documents of the fifteenth- and sixteenth-century Middle East.

When European travelers first encountered the beverage in the coffeehouses of Syria, Egypt, and Turkey in the sixteenth century, the beans from which it was brewed came from terraces in the mountains at the southern tip of the Arabian peninsula, in what is now Yemen. Consequently, when the European botanist Linnaeus began naming and categorizing the flora of the astounding new worlds his colleagues were encountering, he assigned the coffee tree the species name *Coffea arabica.*

Coffea arabica was the only coffee species known to world commerce for several centuries. It still provides the majority of the world's coffees. However, it did not originate in Arabia, as Linnaeus assumed, but in the high forests of central Ethiopia, a fact not confirmed by the Western scientific community until the mid-twentieth century. Well over a hundred species of coffee now have been identified growing wild in various parts of tropical Africa, Asia, and Madagascar. Probably about thirty are cultivated, most on a very small scale. One, *Coffea canephora* or *robusta*, has come to rival *Coffea arabica* in importance in commerce and culture.

No one knows how *Coffea arabica* first came to be cultivated, when, or even where. Some historians assume that it was first cultivated in Yemen, but a strong case has been made that it was first deliberately grown in its botanical home, Ethiopia, and was carried from there to South Arabia as an already domesticated species, perhaps as early as A.D. 575.

It is not clear what sort of drink the first recorded drinkers of hot coffee actually consumed. The coffee bean is the seed of a small, thin-fleshed, sweet fruit. The first hot coffee beverage may not have been brewed from the bean at all. More likely it was made by boiling the lightly toasted husks of the coffee fruit, producing a drink still widely consumed in Yemen under the name *qishr, kishr, kisher* (or several other spellings), and in Europe called *coffee sultan* or *sultana*. Or perhaps both dried fruit and beans were toasted, crushed, and boiled together. The dried husks are very sweet, so any drink involving the husks would be sweet as well as caffeinated.

Considerable speculation has been focused on what finally led someone in Syria, Persia, or possibly Turkey to subject the seeds of the coffee fruit alone to a sufficiently high temperature to induce pyrolysis, thus developing the delicate flavor oils that speak to the palate so eloquently and are undoubtedly responsible for the eventual cultural victory of coffee.

These explanations range from the poetic to the plausible. Muslim legends focus on Sheik Omar, who was exiled to an infertile region of Arabia in about 1260, and according to one version of his legend discovered the benefits of roasted coffee while trying to avoid starvation by making a soup of coffee seeds. Since he found them bitter, he roasted them before boiling them.

Others have claimed that farmers in Yemen or Ethiopia, while burning branches cut from coffee trees to cook their meals, discovered the value in the seeds roasted by this serendipitous process. This theory, which began turning up in coffee literature of the early twentieth century, has a storyteller's rather than a historian's logic.

Ian Bersten, in his provocative history *Coffee Floats, Tea Sinks,* supposes that someone simply discovered that the light roasting given the husks of the coffee fruit to make qishr could be turned up a notch, as it were, to produce a truly roasted coffee bean. He further suggests that the Ottoman Turks, who assumed control of southern Arabia in the mid-sixteenth century, spread the habit of drinking the new kind of roasted coffee in order to make use of a heretofore useless by-product of qishr production, the previously discarded seeds.

Certainly the Ottoman Turks were the main instigators of the spread of coffee drinking and technology, since their expanding empire facilitated cultural and commercial exchange. Bersten also speculates that Syria is the likely location of the first truly roasted coffee, since the Syrians, particularly in the city of Damascus, had developed the technology necessary to produce metal cookware, which in turn facilitated a higher roasting temperature than the earthenware bowls used by the Yemenis.

Furthermore, Bersten suggests that the odor of roasting smoke, which is produced only by pyrolysis and which many people find more enticing than the beverage itself, may have been an incentive for someone to persist in the roasting process and push it beyond the temperature that produces the fruity-smelling qishr.

All such speculations remain impossible to prove or disprove. Seeds and nuts were roasted to improve their taste and digestibility early in history, long before the development of roasted coffee, and possibly someone simply tried the same trick with coffee seeds. Or perhaps some qishr drinker toasting coffee husks and seeds wandered away from the fire too long and came back to a pleasant surprise.

At any rate, by 1550 coffee seeds or beans were definitely being roasted in the true sense of the word in Syria and Turkey, and the spectacular rise of roasted coffee to worldwide prominence in culture and commerce had begun.

Ceremonial Roasting

Early coffee roasting in Arabia was doubtless simple in the extreme. We have no detailed accounts of these earliest of roasting sessions, but they probably resemble the practices still found in Arabia today, and recorded by Europeans like William Palgrave in 1863 in his *Narrative of a Year's Journey Through Central and Eastern Arabia:*

> Without delay Soweylim begins his preparations for coffee. These open by about five minutes of blowing with the bellows and arranging the charcoal till a sufficient heat has been produced.... He then takes a dirty knotted rag out of a niche in the wall close by, and having untied it, empties out of it three or four handfuls of unroasted coffee, the which he places on a little trencher of platted grass, and picks carefully out any blackened grains, or other non-homologous substances, commonly to be found intermixed with the berries when purchased in gross; then, after much cleansing and shaking, he pours the grain so cleansed into a large open iron ladle, and places it over the mouth of the funnel, at the same time blowing the bellows and stirring the grains gently round and round till they crackle, redden, and smoke a little, but carefully withdrawing them from the heat long before they turn black or charred, after the erroneous fashion of Turkey and Europe; after which he puts them to cool a moment on the grass platter.

Among the inhabitants of the Arabian peninsula, roasting, pulverizing, brewing, and drinking the coffee all were (and often still are) performed in one long, leisurely sitting. Both roasting and brewing were carried out over the same small fire. The roasting beans were stirred with an iron rod flattened at one end. After cooling they were dumped into a mortar, where they were pulverized to a coarse powder. The coffee was boiled, usually with some cardamom or saffron added, then strained into cups. It was drunk unsweetened.

Variants of this coffee ritual continue throughout the horn of Africa and the Middle East. Ethiopian and Eritrean immigrants to the United States have carried a version of it to their urban kitchens and living rooms.

From Brown to Black: A New Coffee Cuisine

Attentive readers of the Palgrave passage will note that the Arabians roasted their coffee to a rather light brown color. At an early point in coffee history, probably before 1600, a somewhat different approach to coffee roasting and cuisine developed in Turkey, Syria, and Egypt. The beans were brought to a very dark, almost black color, ground to a very fine powder, using either a millstone or a grinder with metal burrs, and boiled and served with sugar. No spices were added to the cup, and the coffee was not strained, but delivered with some of the powdery grounds still floating in the coffee, suspended in the sweet liquid. It was served in small cups rather than the somewhat larger cups preferred by the Arabians.

The reasons for this change in style of roast, brewing, and serving is not known, but doubtless the very dark roast facilitated grinding the coffee to a fine powder. Lighter roasted beans are tougher in texture and more difficult to pulverize than the more brittle darker roasts. And sugar, a native of India, which had been put into large-scale cultivation relatively recently in the Middle East, helped offset the bitterness of the dark roast and accentuate its sweet undertones. Thus a new technology (the hand grinder with metal burrs), a new, dark roasting style, and the availability of sugar all coincided to contribute to the development of the coffee cuisine we now call Turkish.

Why Turkish? Why not Egyptian, for example, or Syrian? Because this cuisine penetrated Europe via contacts with the Ottoman Turks, first through Venice into northern Italy, and later through the Balkans and Vienna into Central Europe. Early European coffee drinkers all roasted their coffee very dark and drank it in the "Turkish" fashion, boiled with sugar.

Coffee Goes Global

The seventeenth and early eighteenth centuries saw the habit of coffee drinking spread westward across Europe and eastward into India and what is now Indonesia. As a cultivated plant it burst out of Yemen: First a Muslim pilgrim carried it to India, then Europeans took it to Ceylon and Java. From Java they carried it to indoor botanical gardens in Amsterdam and Paris, then as a lucrative new crop to the Caribbean and South America. In a few short decades millions of trees were providing revenue for plantation owners and merchants, and mental fuel for a new generation of philosophers and thinkers gathering in the coffeehouses of London, Paris, and Vienna.

Throughout coffee's spread as one of the new commodity crops that fed the growing global trade network of the seventeenth and eighteenth centuries, it was associated with sugar. Coffee and sugar went hand in hand, both as sister tropical cash crops and as partners in the coffeehouses and coffee cups of the world. Coffee was undoubtedly a less destructive crop than sugar, both to the environment and to workers. It is a small tree typically grown under the shade of larger trees rather than in vast fields, and, unlike sugar, often provided a small cash crop for independent peasant farmers.

Nevertheless, in a global irony, coffee simultaneously became a symbol for both oppression and liberation. It developed as an instrument of social and economic exploitation in the tropics as a plantation elite grew wealthy on the labor of darker-skinned workers, yet simultaneously fueled the intellectual revolution of the European Enlightenment and political revolutions in France and the United States. Coffee and coffeehouses were intimately associated with virtually all of the great cultural and political upheavals of the time.

It was also during the late seventeenth and early eighteenth centuries that Europeans introduced coffee to its second great companion: milk. The ancestor of America's latest favorite, the hot-milk-and-espresso *caffè latte*, was born in Vienna after the Turkish siege of 1683, when Franz Kolschitzky started Vienna's first coffeehouse with coffee left behind by the retreating Turks. Kolschitzky found that in order to woo the Viennese away from their breakfasts of warm beer he had to abandon the Turkish style of coffee brewing, strain the new drink, and serve it with milk.

From Vienna the practice of straining coffee, rather than serving it in Turkish style as a suspension, spread westward through Europe, and with it the custom of serving coffee with hot milk. To this day the line between those European societies that strain their coffee and drink it with milk and those that drink their coffee Turkish-style in a sweet suspension roughly corresponds to the seventeenth- and eighteenth-century border between the Ottoman Empire and Christian Europe. Austrians and Italians, for example, drink their coffee strained and with milk, whereas most coffee drinkers in the Balkans, which remained under the control of the Ottomans until well into the nineteenth century, take their coffee Turkish-style.

Roasting in a Technological Rut

Despite these dramatic developments in coffee drinking and growing during the seventeenth and eighteenth centuries, roasting technology itself changed very little.

The most common approach was a simple carryover from Middle Eastern practice. Beans were put in an iron pan over a fire and stirred until they were brown.

Somewhat more sophisticated devices tumbled the beans inside metal cylinders or globes that were suspended over a fire and turned by hand. Some of these apparatuses could roast several pounds of coffee at a time and were used in coffeehouses and small retail shops; others roasted a pound or less over the embers of home fireplaces. See pages 38–39 and 43 for a sampling of these early roasting devices.

One of the earliest (c. 1650) representations of a small cylindrical coffee roaster, ancestor of the devices that still roast much of the coffee we drink today. It was turned over the hot coals of a brazier or fireplace.

More Unanswerable Questions

Where did Europeans and Americans in the seventeenth and eighteenth centuries roast their coffee? Did they roast it at home or buy it in shops? How dark did they roast it? How might it have tasted when compared to our contemporary roasts?

Only the first two of these questions can be answered with any certainty. Coffee was roasted either in the home, often by servants, or it was roasted in small shops or stalls and sold in bulk like any other produce. There is no evidence that roasting coffee was considered any more difficult or challenging than other kitchen chores. In fact, it appears that, in Europe at least, it was a job often given over to older children.

How well roasted was this coffee? What did it taste like? Iron pans, irregular heat, and children doing the roasting probably meant a technically poor roast: inconsistent and occasionally scorched. The storekeepers probably did better, though not by much.

But again, the coffee was definitely *fresh*. A case certainly could be made that kitchen-roasted coffee in these centuries tasted considerably better than today's instants and cheaper canned coffees.

Roast Style and Geography

Taste in darkness of roast doubtless differed from place to place according to cultural preference, much as it does today. In most of Europe during the sixteenth and seventeenth centuries coffee continued to be roasted in dark, Turkish style. A pamphlet from seventeenth-century England, for example, advises coffee lovers to "take what quantity [of coffee beans] you please and over a charcoal fire, in an old pudding pan or frying pan, keep them always stirring til they be quite black."

At some point, however, tastes in northern Europe—Germany, Scandinavia, and England—modulated to a lighter roast than the rest of Europe, which retained a preference for the somewhat darker roasts deriving from the Turkish tradition. This distinction carried over to the New World: North Americans largely adopted the lighter roasts of the dominant northern European colonists and Latin Americans the darker roasts of their southern European colonizers.

I have yet to come across a plausible explanation as to why northern Europe abandoned the darker roasts of the earlier Turkish-influenced tradition for the later lighter roasts. This shift in roast preference apparently occurred in the late seventeenth and early eighteenth centuries, and it probably was related in some way to the development of the taste for filtered coffee that took place during the same period. Some have connected it to the taste for lighter beverages like tea and beer in northern Europe, which (the theory goes) influenced tastes in coffee roasting and brewing.

Arabia and parts of the horn of Africa retained their original taste for a lighter-roast coffee, drunk with spices but without sugar.

Enter the Industrial Revolution

At the beginning of the nineteenth century most western Europeans and Americans lived in the countryside and made their living through agriculture; by the end of the century most resided in cities and earned their livelihood in industry and services. At the beginning of the century most spent their lives isolated inside an envelope of tradition; by 1900 many were literate and participated in a wider world in which newspapers and advertising profoundly influenced the details of their lives. At the beginning of the century machinery and tools were simple and most power derived from renewable resources like water and wind; by the end complex machinery touched every facet of people's lives, and power overwhelmingly was provided by coal and oil.

Like everything else, coffee was swept along in these changes. As the nineteenth century began, coffee beans were roasted in small, simple machines, either at home or in shops and coffeehouses. By the end of the century the new urban middle class was increasingly buying coffee roasted in large, sophisticated machines and sold in packages by brand name.

Naturally this last development was uneven. Among industrial-ized nations the United States led in replacing home roasting with packaged preroasted and preground coffee. Germany and Great Britain were close behind, with France, Italy, and industrializing nations elsewhere hanging on to older, small-scale roasting traditions.

An example of one of the earliest advertisements intended to woo people away from home roasting to packaged, brand-name coffees is reproduced on page 27. This sort of advertising appeared at a time when increasing numbers of Americans and Europeans found them-selves traveling farther and farther to their places of employment. In working-class families women as well as men worked away from home, and toward the end of the century somewhat better-off families, who once employed live-in servants to take care of tasks like coffee roasting, were forced to do it themselves. In this context it is easy to see why people might begin to prefer the costlier but more convenient option of preroasted coffee.

New preferences for store-bought bread and preroasted coffee also were driven by the myth of progress that infatuated the indus-trialized world throughout the nineteenth and early twentieth cen-turies. Packaged preroasted coffee was modern, clean, fashionable, and with-it. Roasting your own coffee was dirty, clumsy, grubby, and old-fashioned, something only your ignorant country cousins did.

The Pursuit of Consistency

With advertising and brand names came the need for a consis-tent, recognizable product. When a consumer bought your coffee in its fancy package, it was important to make the coffee inside the package taste the same way now as it did last week. The new com-mercial coffee roasters pursued consistency in both the green coffee they roasted and in the roast itself.

Consistency in green coffee was facilitated in several ways. The international coffee trade became better organized and more sophis-ticated in the language and categories it used to describe coffees and carry on its business. Countries where coffee was grown introduced complex standards for grading beans. The art of blending developed: Professionals learned how to juggle coffees from different crops and regions in order to maintain a consistent taste while controlling costs.

Meanwhile the American coffee industry developed a trade lan-guage for degree or style of roast: cinnamon, light, medium, high, city,

Based on a turn-of-the-century photograph, this drawing depicts one of the many itinerant coffee roasters who with their simple equipment roamed the cities and towns of nineteenth- and early twentieth-century France, setting up in the street and roasting coffee for neighborhood households. With his left hand he is turning the ball-shaped roasting chamber above a charcoal fire; in his right he holds a metal hook used to open the door in the roasting ball to check the color of the beans. The boxlike wooden object at his feet is his cooling tray. When he judged the coffee properly roasted, he flipped the ball on its hinged frame up and out of the top of the stove and over the cooling tray, into which it deposited its charge of hot beans.

full city, dark, heavy. Firms settled on a roast style and rigorously attempted to maintain it.

Tireless Tinkering: Nineteenth-Century Roasting Technology

It is never clear whether changes in technology drive changes in society or vice versa, but certainly the two went hand in hand in transforming nineteenth-century coffee roasting from a small-scale, personal act to a large-scale, industrial procedure, fed by advertising and mass-marketing techniques. The consistency in roast style demanded by brand-name marketing could only be obtained through a more refined roasting technology.

The restless innovation of the Industrial Revolution, the tireless entrepreneurial tinkering aimed at coming up with yet another machine, still one more money-making technical wrinkle, claimed all aspects of coffee during the nineteenth century, from roasting through brewing. Proposals for new—or almost new—coffee makers, coffee grinders, and coffee roasters streamed through the doors of patent offices in industrializing countries. Although only a few of the many patents had significant impact, enough did to totally transform roasting technology over the course of the century.

Coffee continued to be roasted in hollow cylinders or globes, but the cylinders and globes dramatically increased in size as coffee roasting moved from kitchens and small storefront shops to large roasting factories. See page 26 for a look at the interior of an American coffee-roasting plant from the mid-nineteenth century.

The roasting drums were now turned by machine, first by steam, then near the end of the century by electricity. Similarly, roasting heat was first provided by coal or wood, then by natural gas. By the end of the century a lively debate developed between adherents of "direct" gas roasting, which meant that the flame and the hot gases were literally present inside the roasting chamber, and "indirect" gas roasting, which meant that heat was applied only to the outside of the roasting chamber and sucked through the chamber by means of a fan or air pump.

Further technical innovations focused on two problems: (1) controlling the timing or duration of the roast with precision, and (2) achieving an even roast from bean to bean and around the circumference of each individual bean.

First the timing issue. As the drums and globes of commercial roasting machines grew larger it became more and more difficult to cool the large masses of roasting coffee with any exactness because the beans continued to roast from their own internal heat long after being dumped from the machine or removed from the heat source.

Solutions in the early part of the century tended to focus on ways of dumping the beans quickly and easily. With the Carter Pull-Out machines pictured in the engraving on page 26, for example, the selling point was exactly that: The roasting drum could be pulled out of the oven and easily emptied. However, as can be seen in the illustration, the beans still had to be stirred manually to hasten cooling.

Starting in 1867 fans or air pumps were introduced to automate the cooling. The beans were dumped into large pans or trays. While machine-driven paddles stirred the beans, fans pulled cool air through them, both reducing their surface temperature and carrying away the smoke produced by the freshly roasted beans.

The second technical problem addressed by late-nineteenth-century innovation was the question of even roasting. At the beginning of the century most roasting drums and globes were simple hollow chambers. The beans tended to collect in a relatively stable mass at the bottom of the turning drum or globe. Consequently some beans remained at the bottom of the pile in close contact with the hot metal of the drum and tended to scorch or roast darker than those at the top of the shifting mass. Furthermore the coating of oil produced by the roast often caused beans to stick to the hot metal walls of the roasting chamber.

Starting in the nineteenth century, vanes or blades were added to the inside of the roasting chamber, which tossed the coffee as the drum or globe turned, facilitating a more even roast. And in 1864 Jabez Burns, an American roasting-technology innovator, further resolved the problem of dumping the beans by developing a double-screw arrangement of vanes inside the roasting drum that worked the beans up and down the length of the cylinder as it turned. The operator then had only to open the door of the roasting cylinder and the beans, rather than heading back away from the door for another trip up the cylinder, simply tumbled out into the cooling tray.

But the most effective answer to uneven roasting came toward the end of the century. To supplement the usual heat applied to the outside of the drum, hot air was drawn *through* the drum by a fan or air pump, often the same fan or pump used to suck air through the beans

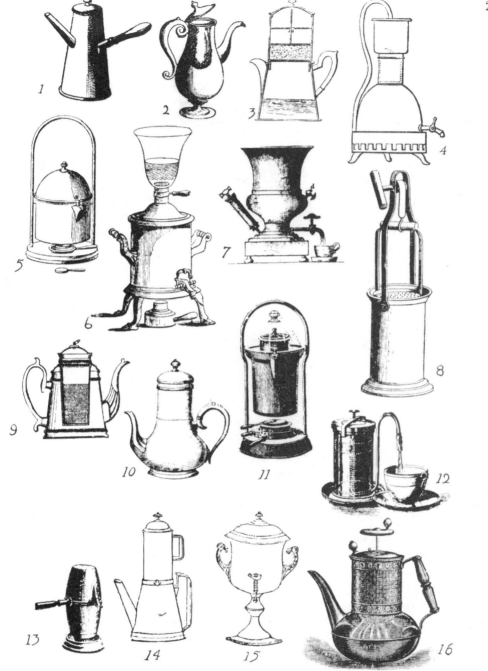

This nineteenth-century illustration suggests the outpouring of invention that was lavished on the simple act of coffee brewing during the early Industrial Revolution. Similar ingenuity was bestowed on coffee roasting. Scores of almost identical home-roasting devices were patented, as well as numerous variations on shop and factory machines.

The interior of an American roasting plant in the mid-nineteenth century. Heat was provided by coal; brick ovens entirely surrounded the roasting drums, distributing heat more evenly around the drums than did earlier designs that heated the drums from the bottom only. The drums were perforated to vent the roasting smoke. These Carter Pull-Out roasters were turned by belts connecting to steam power, but were "pulled out" of the ovens by hand. The beans were dumped into wooden trays, where they were cooled by stirring with shovels.

to cool them. The combination of moving air and vanes tossing the coffee meant the coffee was roasted more by contact with hot air than through contact with hot metal, improving both the consistency and the speed of the roast. Furthermore, efforts were made to deliver heat evenly around the entire circumference of the drum rather than only at the bottom, usually by enclosing the drum inside a second metal wall and circulating the heat between this wall and the outside of the drum.

The sum total of these innovations—gas heat directed evenly around the drum, a means of rapidly and precisely dumping the beans, vanes inside the drum, and air pumps to suck hot air through the roasting chamber and room-temperature air through the cooling beans—produced the basic configuration of the classic drum roaster.

It is a configuration that endures today as the fundamental form of most smaller-scale roasting equipment. See pages 52–53 for an illustrated description of a representative drum roaster.

Of course there were (and are) many variations to this essential technology. Some turn-of-the-century machines put the gas flame inside the drum, for example. Most larger systems today spray the hot beans with a short burst of water to decisively kick off the cooling process, an approach called *water quenching* as opposed to the pure *air quenching* described earlier.

In the nineteenth and early twentieth centuries, coating the hot beans with sugar to help preserve them was a popular practice. Today *sugar glazing* of coffee beans is practiced only in some regions of Latin America and Europe.

Throughout these decades of change some roasters stuck stubbornly to earlier technologies, as they still do today. Roasters in places as diverse as Japan, Brazil, and the United States continue to use wood or charcoal to roast their coffee, for example. They or their

An advertisement aimed at getting Americans of the 1870s to give up home roasting for packaged coffees. Arbuckles Brothers pioneered pre-roasted, brand-name coffee. Note the contrast between the up-to-date woman on the left, fashionably dressed and holding a package of pre-roasted coffee, and her distracted old-fashioned friend, tied to her stove and messing up the kitchen with coffee smoke.

clients value the slow roast and the smoky nuance imparted to the beans by the process.

Nevertheless, the indirectly heated drum roaster using a convection system drawing hot air through the turning drum remains the norm today for all but the largest roasting apparatus.

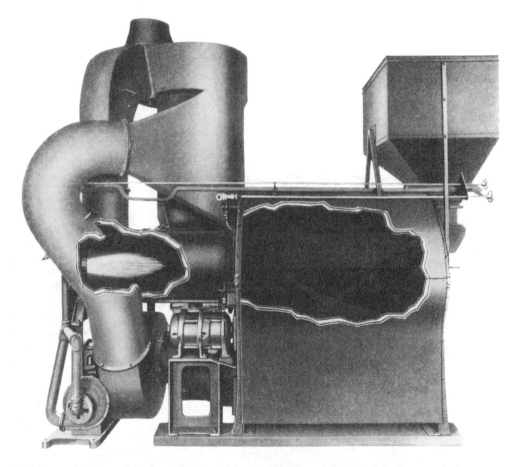

The Jabez Burns Thermalo roaster of 1934. Previous machines supplemented the heat applied to the outside of the roasting drum with relatively gentle currents of hot air drawn through the drum. The Burns machine dispensed with the heat outside the drum, instead relying on a high-velocity blast of hot air roaring through the drum, thus roasting the coffee more by contact with hot air than by contact with hot metal. Burns machines like this one are still used in many medium-sized American roasting establishments. The principle pioneered by the Thermalo reached its ultimate development in today's fluid-bed machines, which lift as well as roast the beans in the same rapidly moving, vertical column of hot air.

Twentieth-Century Innovations: Hot Air Only

Obviously the twentieth century could not leave coffee-roasting technology alone. The goal of roasting coffee beans as they fly through the air rather than rattling off hot metal or sizzling in a gas flame received two additional boosts in the middle years of the century.

In 1934 the Jabez Burns company developed a machine (the first model was called the Thermalo; see the preceding page) that applied no heat whatsoever to the drum itself, instead relying entirely on a powerful stream of hot air howling through the drum. This arrangement permitted the use of a lower air temperature during roasting, since the rapidly moving air stripped the beans of their envelope of roasting gas and made the actual heat transfer from air to bean more efficient. Adherents of the new system argued that lower roasting temperatures and relatively rapid roasting burn off fewer flavor oils and produce a more aromatic coffee.

Also in the 1930s the first roasting device appeared that quite logically dispensed with the roasting drum altogether and instead used the same powerful column of hot air that roasted the beans to also agitate them. Such *fluid- (or fluidized-) bed* roasters work essentially like today's household hot-air corn poppers; the stream of hot air simultaneously tumbles and roasts the beans. The bed of beans seethes like fluid, hence the name. Fluid-bed roasters offer the same technical advantages as the Burns Thermalo machine: the rapidly moving air permits a lower roast temperature and a faster roast, theoretically driving off fewer flavor oils.

In the United States today the most widely used fluid-bed designs are the work of Michael Sivetz, an influential American coffee technician and writer. In the most popular Sivetz design the beans are forced upward along a vertical wall by the stream of hot air, then cascade back down again in a continuous rotation. See page 46 for an illustrated description of one style of Sivetz roaster.

Several other fluid-bed designs have been manufactured over the past fifty years, and more continue to enter the market. Some are simple variations on the original patents from fifty years ago, in which hot air rising from the bottom of a funnel-shaped roasting chamber creates a sort of fountain of beans that seethes upward in the middle before tumbling back down the sides of the chamber. Other designs, like Australian Ian Bersten's Roller Roaster and the Burns System 90 centrifugal, packed-bed roaster, are efforts to genuinely rethink the original fluid-bed principle. Still others, like the recently developed Louisville

Roaster, are *display roasters* that emphasize the drama of the procedure by enclosing the seething beans in glass. The idea is to draw customers into the store by flaunting roasting's technological and gourmet intrigue. All of the newer small fluid-bed shop roasters attempt to simplify and automate the roasting process as much as possible.

Electrified Roasting

Electricity came into use late in the nineteenth century to turn drums and pump air through conventional roasters. Electricity has not achieved great success as a heat source for large-scale roasting, however. As any cook knows, electric heat responds sluggishly to command compared to gas. Gas also is usually cheaper. For these reasons it has remained the preferred heat source in most larger shop and factory roasting installations.

Nevertheless, several shop roasting devices manufactured in the early part of the century provided roasting heat with electrical elements, and electricity continues in use in many small-scale roasting installations today. The Rair Aerabica roaster, which encloses the familiar roasting drum inside a commercial-strength convection oven, is a case in point, as are most of the small fluid-bed shop roasters described earlier.

Infrared and Microwaves

The use of electromagnetic waves or radiation to roast coffee has had mixed success.

Infrared is radiation with a wavelength greater than visible light but shorter than microwaves. It is used in outdoor-café heaters, portable home heaters, and similar applications.

The first infrared roasting machines appeared in the 1950s. Today one of the leading small American shop roasters, the Diedrich roaster, uses infrared heat. Like most drum roasters, the Diedrich machine combines heat applied to the outside of the roasting drum with currents of hot air drawn through it to roast the coffee. Unlike conventional drum roasters, however, the heat is supplied by radiating, gas-heated ceramic tiles. Metal heat exchangers apply some of the radiant heat to warm the air pulled through the drum. Proponents of the Diedrich machine admire its relative energy efficiency, low emissions, and clean-tasting roast.

So far, efforts to use microwaves to roast coffee have not proven practical, but the idea obviously will continue to be pressed, and it may well be that someone will break through with a practical system as the turn of the century approaches.

Roasting Without End: The Continuous Roaster

For large roasting companies time is money, and emptying beans from the roaster and reloading with more beans takes time. Such economic motives lay behind still another twentieth-century development, the *continuous roaster*, in which the roasting process never stops until the machine is turned off.

The most common continuous-roasting design elongates the typical roasting drum and puts a sort of screw arrangement inside it. As the drum turns, the screwlike vanes transport the coffee from one end of the drum to the other in a slow, one-way trip. Hot air is circulated across the drum at the front end and cool air at the far end. The movement of the beans through the drum is timed so that green coffee entering the drum is first roasted then cooled by the time it tumbles out at the end of its journey. Variations of this principle continue to be employed in machines used today in many large commercial roasting establishments. See page 49 for an illustrated description.

The fluid-bed principle has been pressed into service for continuous roasters as well. In these designs hot air simultaneously roasts and stirs large batches of coffee, which drop into a cooling chamber as soon as they are roasted, to be followed immediately by another batch of green coffee and still another, in continuous succession.

Conventional roasting machines that need to be stopped completely to be emptied and reloaded are now called *batch roasters* to distinguish them from continuous designs. Most specialty or fancy coffee roasting establishments have stayed with batch roasters. If you are roasting a Kenyan coffee in the morning, a Sumatran at midday, and an espresso blend in the afternoon, the single-minded persistence of the continuous design makes no sense. On the other hand, large commercial roasting companies that roast a similar blend of coffee the same way every day find the consistent conveyor-belt approach embodied in such machines practical and desirable.

Chaff and Roasting Smoke

Some developments in nineteenth- and twentieth-century coffee-roasting technology have little to do with improving taste or the bottom line, but instead respond to safety and environmental concerns.

The earliest of these issues to be faced involved roasting chaff. Green coffee arrives at the roaster with small, dry flakes of the inner-most skin, or silverskin, still clinging to the bean. During roasting most of these flakes separate from the beans and float wherever air currents take them. They can be dangerous if they settle in one place and ignite, and are always annoying.

Recall that in the late nineteenth century fans were put into service to pull hot air through the roasting drum. This advance led to the development of the *cyclone*, a large, hollow, cone-shaped object that typically sits behind the roasting chamber. After the hot air is pulled from the roasting drum it is allowed to circulate inside the cyclone, where most of the chaff it has been carrying settles out. The chaff-free air and smoke then continue up and out of the chimney while the chaff collects at the base of the cyclone, where it can be removed and disposed of.

In the twentieth century the persistent odor of the roasting smoke and its potential pollutants became an issue. Technology came to the rescue with afterburners and catalytic devices that remove a good deal of the roasting by-products from the exiting gases. Fuel was often conserved by recirculating at least a portion of the hot roasting air back through the roasting chamber.

A Revolution in Measurement and Control

As the twenty-first century approaches, there are signs that roasting technology may be undergoing still another revolution. Barring some breakthrough in the use of microwaves, it seems unlikely that the basic technologies for applying heat to the beans and keeping them moving will change. What is changing is the way the roast is monitored and controlled.

Traditionalists: Nose and Eye

Until recently small-scale roasting remained not too far removed from the hands-on approach of the Neapolitans cranking their *abbrus-tulaturo* on their balconies as recalled by Eduardo De Filippo in Chapter 1. I know one respected specialty coffee roaster who monitors the roast by smelling the smoke, for example. When it turns full and rounded he concludes that the roast is approaching its optimum development.

More typically, traditional roasters rely on the eye, carefully observing the developing color of the roast by means of a little instrument called a trier, which they insert through a hole in the front of the roasting machine to collect a sample of the tumbling beans. The decision when to stop the roast is based on the color of the beans read in light of experience. Adjustments to the temperature inside the roast chamber also may be made on the basis of experience, experience both with roasting generally and with the idiosyncrasies of specific coffees.

For a traditionalist, roasting is an art in the old sense of the word: a hands-on experience unfolding again and again in the arena of memory and the senses.

Science Sneaks Up on Art

What was once a matter of art and the human senses, however, is increasingly becoming a matter of science and instrumentation, in which individual memory is replaced by an externalized, collective memory of numbers and graphs.

Several instruments and controls are making this change possible.

The first is a simple device that measures the approximate internal temperature of the roasting beans. Usually called a *thermocouple* or *heat probe*, it is an electronic thermometer, whose sensing end is placed inside the roasting chamber so that it is entirely surrounded by the moving mass of beans. Although the air temperature inside the roasting chamber is different from the temperature of the beans, the beans tend to insulate the sensor from the air and transmit an approximate reading of their inner, collective heat to a display on the outside of the machine.

Once the chemical changes associated with roasting set in, the internal heat of the beans becomes a reasonably precise indicator of how far along the roast is. Think of the little thermometers that pop out of roasted turkeys when they're properly done. The inner temperature of roasting beans is a similar indicator of "doneness," or degree of roast. Thus the electronic thermometer can be used in place of the eye to gauge when to conclude the roast or make adjustments to the temperature inside the roast chamber. A chart matching approximate internal temperature with degree or style of roast appears on pages 68–69. With some contemporary roasting machinery it is possible to set the instrumentation to trigger the cooling cycle automatically when the beans have reached a predetermined internal temperature.

A second important control links the temperature inside the roasting chamber with the heat supply, automatically modifying the amount of heat to maintain a steady, predetermined temperature inside the chamber. This linkage is desirable because once the beans reach pyrolysis they emit their own heat, raising the temperature in the roasting chamber. If the amount of heat applied from outside the chamber remains uniform, as it does with the simpler conventional apparatus, then the heat inside the chamber begins to accelerate near the end of the roast, fed by the new heat supplied by the chemical changes in the beans. According to some roast philosophies, these spiraling, uncontrolled temperatures may roast the beans too quickly, burning off aromatics and weakening the structure of the bean.

A third instrument is the *near-infrared spectrophotometer*. This device, often called an *Agtron* after its manufacturers and developer, measures certain wavelengths of "color" or electromagnetic energy not visible to the human eye, but which correlate particularly well with the degree of roast. Furthermore, the Agtron is not deceived by the changing quality of ambient light or by other sources of human fallibility like bad moods or talkative coworkers. The near-infrared spectrophotometer not only measures its narrow, telltale band of energy with consistency and precision, but translates it into a number as well. Thus two people thousands of miles apart can compare the development of their roasts by exchanging the readings on their instruments.

It has long been known that denser and/or moister coffees are slower to reach a given roast style than lighter or drier beans. Today's technically inclined roaster takes precise measurements of bean density and sets roast-chamber temperature and other variables to compensate for these differences according to a quantified system. The

This billboard from the 1930s dramatizes how preroasted, preground coffee was associated with modernity and progress in the early twentieth century.

traditional roaster can only approximate such adjustments based on past experience with the behavior of a given coffee in the roaster.

Finally, the velocity of the convection currents of air and gases moving through the roasting chamber can be controlled with great precision in some contemporary roasting equipment. Traditional roasters have always been able to control air currents in their drum roasters by adjusting a damper, much as we control convection currents in our home fireplaces and wood stoves. But again, this control was approximate rather than quantifiable and precise.

Thus today's systematic roaster has four to five quantifiable variables with which to work: original moisture content and density of the beans, temperature in the roasting chamber, internal temperature of the roasting beans, precisely measured color of the roasting beans, and (with some equipment) air velocity in the roasting chamber. Add in careful compensation for environmental factors like ambient temperature, altitude, and barometric pressure, and figures provided by these four or five variables can describe the progress and conclusion of a given roasting session for a given coffee, replacing the ear, nose, eye, and memory with a set of hard data. With the use of computers, complex settings can be established to vary the temperature and other conditions inside the roast chamber on an almost second-by-second basis, permitting subtle modifications of the final taste of the roast, an approach called *profile roasting* by its proponents. Older, blander coffees can be made to taste somewhat more complex, for example, and rough or acidy coffees can be tamed and made smoother and sweeter.

But It Still Needs to Be Tasted

You may have patiently followed all of the preceding, or simply skimmed it to get to the punch line. Either way you can see how the use of instrumentation permits translating what was once an intuitive system held in the memory and nervous system of the roaster to a complex but precise series of numbers.

One human sense that hopefully will never become obsolete is taste. For even if the day arrives when roasting is performed entirely on the basis of system and number, the roaster (or roastmaster as he/she is increasingly called in these upscale days) still will need to taste the coffee when it comes out of the roasting apparatus and make some informed adjustments to those numbers, based on personal preference and roasting philosophy. Thus the variety of taste achieved by different approaches to roasting may continue to surprise our palates and enrich the culture and connoisseurship of coffee. Roasting, perhaps, will remain art as well as science.

Social History: Quality Makes a Comeback

To conclude, let's return to the social history of roasting and bring it to its rather surprising conclusion in the twentieth century.

Although preroasted, preground coffee sold under brand names claimed more and more of the market in industrialized Europe and America during the first half of the twentieth century, older customs hung on. In southern Europe many people continued to roast their coffee at home well into the 1960s, and even in the United States small storefront roasting shops survived in urban neighborhoods.

As the century wore on, however, the trend toward convenience and standardization accelerated. By the 1960s packaged coffee identified by brand name dominated the urbanized world. Coffee was sold not only preroasted and preground, but in the case of soluble coffees, prebrewed. I recall visiting two of the world's most famous coffee-growing regions in the 1970s and finding only instant coffee served in restaurants and cafés. Most Americans and Europeans, who were now called *consumers*, had forgotten that coffee could be roasted at home, or even that it could be ground at home. Coffee doubtless appeared in their consciousness, perhaps even in their dreams, as round cans or bottles with familiar logos on the sides.

The simple process of home roasting became a lost art, pursued in industrialized societies only by a handful of cranky individualists and elsewhere by isolated rural people who roasted their own coffee as much from economic necessity as from habit or tradition.

Canned coffee became a favorite product to offer at great savings to lure people into large stores. The tendency to use coffee as a loss-leader helped make it one of the most cost-sensitive food products of the 1950s and '60s and understandably undercut the quality of the coffee inside those colorful cans. Commercial canned blends that were reasonably flavorful at the close of World War II became flat and lifeless by the end of the 1960s.

At that point, indicated in Chapter 1, a new phase of the coffee story began, a countermovement to the march toward uniformity and convenience at the cost of quality and variety. The few small shops that still roasted their own coffee and sold it in bulk provided a foundation for a revival of quality coffees that has gone far to transform coffee-consuming habits in the United States and many other parts of the industrialized world.

This revival is usually called the specialty-coffee movement. Thus the end of the twentieth century is witnessing a return to the coffee roasting and selling practices that dominated at its beginning, with people buying their coffee in bulk and grinding it themselves before brewing. Perhaps the United States, which led the world down the superhighway of convenience, may be pointing it back along the slower road toward quality and authenticity.

From Gourmet Ghetto to Shopping Mall

However, a countertrend toward a new kind of standardization seems to be setting in. The specialty-coffee movement began in the 1960s with small roasters selling their coffee as fresh as possible to neighborhood customers. However, specialty coffee has now moved out of gourmet ghettos and into suburban shopping malls. As it has, the stakes have risen. Neighborhood roasters have become regional chains, and regional chains have sold stock and gone national.

Today your neighborhood specialty-coffee store may well be one of a chain of fifty, or in the extraordinary case of Starbucks, one of hundreds. Starbucks buys coffee of impeccably high quality, but roasts it in two large plants and distributes it to a vast network of virtually identical retail outlets across the country.

Quirky and Individualistic

Starbucks is in many ways a happy marriage between the quality-conscious idealism of the specialty-coffee movement and rigorous corporate power and discipline. Nevertheless it does not entirely represent the world of coffee as I would like to see it enter the twenty-first century: quirky and individualistic, with local roasters selling their own styles of coffee in their own neighborhoods, a world full of choice and surprises.

For those who really love coffee, the moment may have come to leave both cans *and* enormous coffee-store chains behind and enjoy coffee as people did before the advent of brand names, chain stores, and advertising: by roasting your own.

A Visual History of Roasting Machines

Home Roasters

For the first several hundred years of coffee history home roasters were the only kind of roaster. They remained a standard kitchen accessory until the early twentieth century.

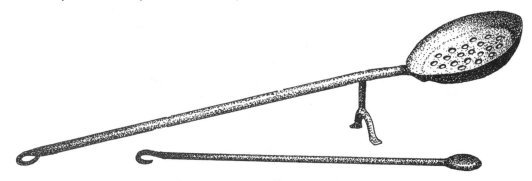

Iraqi Roasting Pan, Sixteenth Century

This simple implement projected over a small fire or the smoldering coals of a brazier, supported by the elongated handle and the two little legs. The bottom of the pan is perforated, and the beans were stirred with the long-handled spoon. According to coffee historian William Ukers, roasters like this one were in use in Iraq by the early sixteenth century.

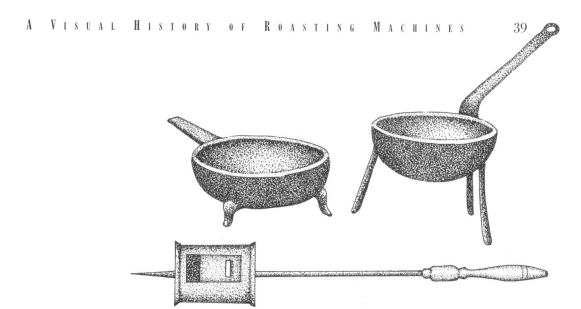

American Fireplace Roasters, Eighteenth Century

These three devices are typical of those used to roast coffee in fireplaces in the seventeenth and eighteenth centuries. The two round-bottomed pans on legs were called spiders. Much of the shop and commercial roasting apparatus in use today evolved from the simple cylinder pictured below the spiders, the point of which rested on an andiron or chink in the fireplace wall while someone (probably a servant or child) dutifully twirled it. Coffee was loaded through the little sliding door on the side of the cylinder.

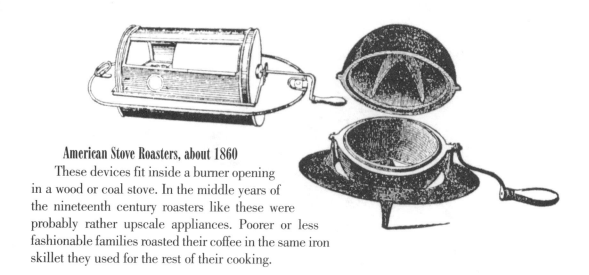

American Stove Roasters, about 1860

These devices fit inside a burner opening in a wood or coal stove. In the middle years of the nineteenth century roasters like these were probably rather upscale appliances. Poorer or less fashionable families roasted their coffee in the same iron skillet they used for the rest of their cooking.

Italian Spirit-Lamp Roaster, Early Nineteenth Century

The glass cylinder of this decorative tabletop roaster usefully permits the operator to observe the developing color of the beans. A spirit lamp furnishes heat.

European Electric Home Roaster, Early Twentieth Century

An electric element in the base provides heat in this countertop roaster. Despite the decline in home roasting in the early twentieth century, a number of devices like this one were marketed in Europe and Japan.

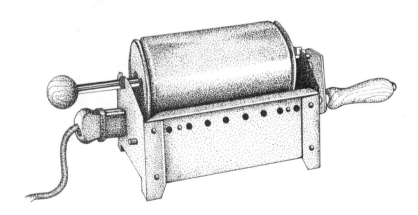

Electric Fluid-Bed Home Roaster, 1980s

This little appliance reflects an effort to use the elegantly simple technology of the fluid bed to revive the practice of home roasting. A column of hot air rises from the base of the device, roasting and seething the beans inside the narrow cylinder that protrudes necklike from the base. The element that sits like a head atop the roasting chamber diverts and collects the chaff that otherwise would float out of the top of the unit.

The AromaRoast was imported from Hong Kong by the Melitta Corporation during the 1980s. Apparently its technology conflicted with claims of American patent holders, whose representatives managed to drive it off the United States market. Perhaps this was just as well, since the AromaRoast was relatively underpowered, roasted very little coffee per session, and did not permit the operator to visually monitor bean color. See page 127 for an illustration of the Sirocco, a much better designed (and more expensive) home fluid-bed roaster imported from Germany during the same period.

Electric Fluid-Bed Home Roaster, Late 1990s

Patent drawing for a fluid-bed home roaster proposed by American inventors Harold Gell and Brian Porto. A group of investors is intent on bringing out an inexpensive home roasting device based on the Gell-Porto patent and other Gell patents consolidated by entrepreneur Steven Pitock. The product that finally hits the shelves in late 1997 probably will differ only in detail from this drawing.

The Gell-Porto design works (and looks) much like the hot-air corn poppers recommended for coffee roasting

elsewhere in this book. Concealed inside the base is a cylindrical roasting chamber. Hot air issuing from louvers in the sides of the bottom third of that chamber rotates the roasting beans in a circular pattern. Cooling is accomplished as it is in virtually all small fluid-bed apparatus: The heating element is turned off while the fan continues to seethe the beans with room-temperature air. In the Gell-Porto prototype the cooling cycle can be activated either manually based on visual observation of the roasting beans, or automatically by setting the mechanical timer pictured near the bottom of the device. The upper part of the roasting chamber is glass and can be removed for cleaning. A chaff collector sits atop the roasting chamber.

Coffee-Roasting Accessory for Hot-Air Corn Poppers, Late 1990s

Patent drawings for the MacCochran roasting adaptor, an innovative device designed to assist in transforming a hot-air corn popper into a coffee roaster. Its patent holder and designer David M. Cochran expects it to debut sometime in late 1996 for under twenty dollars. You don't need to wait for the MacCochran adaptor to roast coffee in a hot-air corn popper, by the way. As I indicate on pages 154–158, all that is required is the right design popper and a bowl to catch the chaff. Nevertheless, the attractive MacCochran adaptor both simplifies and embellishes the roasting process. Fabricated of brass, it slips inside the top of the popping (or roasting) chamber, in effect replacing the popper's plastic hood. A screen opening in the side of the adaptor collects the chaff (static electricity makes the chaff stick to the screen), while the transparent top permits you to look down into the popping/ roasting chamber to keep an eye on roast color. You terminate the roast by unplugging the popper, removing the MacCochran adaptor, and dumping the hot beans in a bowl or colander as described on page 156. Simply tapping the adaptor causes it to drop its load of chaff into the sink or trash container.

Shop Roasters

Shop, retail, or micro roasters are small- to medium-size machines used to roast coffee in stores and cafés. Most coffee not roasted in the home was prepared in shop roasters until the early twentieth century, when factory roasting and packaged preground coffees overwhelmed the market. In the late twentieth century shop roasting is making a comeback as consumers in the United States and other industrialized countries rediscover the pleasure of genuinely fresh coffee.

American Shop Roaster, Eighteenth Century

Probably used in either a shop or coffeehouse, this little device is a simple elaboration on the cylinder roasters used in home fireplaces in the seventeenth and eighteenth centuries. It was placed inside a fireplace over the embers and turned by hand.

British Shop Roasters, Eighteenth Century

The machines illustrated below were advances over the simpler fireplace designs in two respects. They were self-contained, with roasting heat provided by charcoal in the boxes beneath the drums, and they incorporated a hood that helped distribute heat around the entire circumference of the roasting drum.

American Shop Roaster, 1862

This design, dating from 1862 and manufactured by E. J. Hyde of Philadelphia, is typical of more advanced mid-nineteenth-century shop roasters. It incorporated a swing-out roasting drum that facilitated dumping the coffee for cooling and vanes inside the drum that tossed the coffee as the drum turned. Heat continued to be provided by a coal fire under the drum, and the drum was turned by hand.

French Gas Roaster, 1890s

According to William Ukers, the first patent for the use of gas to provide heat for coffee roasting was filed in France in 1877. Today gas continues to roast most of the world's coffee. This gas-fired roaster, patented by M. Postulart in 1888, retains the globular roasting chamber to which the French remained loyal long after the Germans, British, and Americans had unanimously gone over to cylindrical designs. The hot roasted coffee was dumped by gravity from the globular roasting chamber down through a funnel to a cylindrical cooling chamber in the base, and from there into the drawer at the bottom of the machine.

German Shop Roaster, 1907

In the German Perfekt roaster from the first decade of the twentieth century, power is supplied by a belt connected to the pulley protruding at the left. This power turns the drum, and through a system of gears (visible at bottom right) rotates a set of paddles inside the circular cooling tray at the front of the roaster. These paddles agitate the beans and assist in their cooling.

Heat is provided by gas. An air pump, located in the base of the machine and powered by the descending belt at the left, pulls hot roasting air through and around the drum, insuring a more even distribution of heat and faster roasting than could be obtained in earlier machines, in which only the metal of the drum itself was heated. These air currents also dispose of roasting smoke and chaff, the fine paperlike flakes of skin that adhere to green coffee beans. Finally, the pump, by moving fresh air through perforations at the bottom of the cooling tray, assists the turning paddles inside the tray to cool the roasted beans.

In machines of this kind the progress of the roast is monitored by inserting a little pointed scoop called a trier through a small opening in the front of the machine. The trier collects small samples of the tumbling beans, which are then examined for their color until judged ready, and the operator trips a lever sending the roasted beans pouring out into the cooling tray.

Although electronic instrumentation and various refinements were added as the century progressed, machines similar to this one have dominated small-scale coffee roasting throughout the twentieth century.

Small German Shop Roaster, Early Twentieth Century

Fashionably streamlined, compact little devices like the one on the left sat in the windows or near the front doors of many small shops in Germany and other European countries during the 1920s and '30s, enticing passersby with the odor of freshly roasting coffee. It worked almost exactly like the previously described machine.

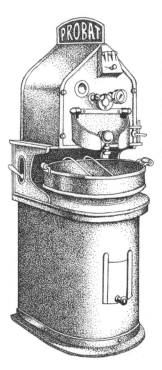

Cross-Section of Fluid-Bed Shop Roaster, 1980s

Fluid-bed machines use the same powerful stream of hot air to simultaneously heat and agitate, or fluidize, the beans. In the design by American Michael Sivetz illustrated here, a column of hot air rises from the base of the machine through a sieve, driving the beans up the wall of the roasting chamber until they cascade back down again to the base in a continuous, fountainlike movement. A thermocouple or heat probe roughly measures the internal temperature of the beans, enabling the operator to conclude the roast on the basis of bean temperature rather than color. The beans are then diverted into a separate chamber, where a column of room-temperature air cools them.

There have been numerous other fluid-bed designs over the past fifty years, all similar in basic principle but varying how the air column and rotation of the beans is managed. Many incorporate a window or glass tube in the roast chamber to add interest to the rather bland-looking machine exteriors. Small fluid-bed roasters also introduced greater automation to the roast procedure, with sophisticated electronic controls making it possible to "instruct" the machine to terminate the roast when the thermocouple indicates that a predetermined bean temperature has been reached.

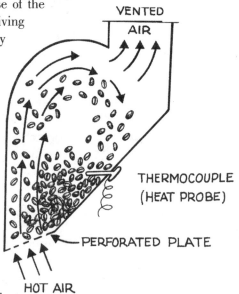

VENTED AIR

THERMOCOUPLE (HEAT PROBE)

PERFORATED PLATE

HOT AIR

Factory Roasters

In the United States the first packaged coffees reached the expanding shelves of stores soon after the Civil War. By the end of World War II preroasted and preground coffees prepared in giant factories completely dominated the North American market. The technology of large roasting devices variously called plant, factory, or commercial roasters developed in parallel to this standardizing, centralizing trend. During the mid- to late-nineteenth century factory roasters were simply larger versions of shop machines, but near the end of the century the first continuous roasting devices were developed, an approach that in one form or another continues to dominate large-scale coffee roasting.

British Factory Roaster, 1848

The Dakin roaster pictured here was a more sophisticated version of the American Carter Pull-Out machines appearing in the engraving on page 26. As with the American machines, the drum was turned by steam power transmitted via pulleys, and was enclosed inside a brick oven. In the Dakin design, however, the drum was surrounded by a second inner metal shell to protect it from direct heat, and the pull-out mechanism was more elegant than the simple arrangement of the American machine.

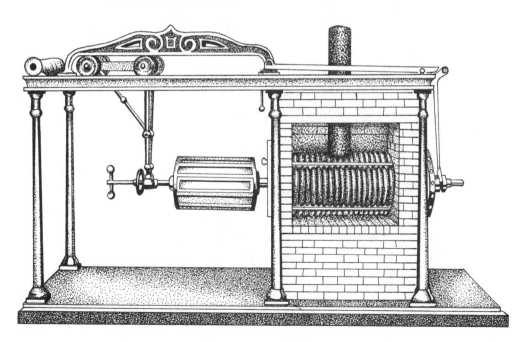

American Small Factory Roaster, 1864

The Jabez Burns roaster of 1864 introduced a double-screw arrangement that worked the coffee in a continuous forward-and-back movement inside the roasting cylinder. This innovation not only distributed the coffee in the cylinder more consistently than did earlier arrangements of vanes, but—more importantly—would work the coffee out the front of the cylinder when the door was opened. Most twentieth-century drum roasters propel the roasted coffee out of the drum using a similar arrangement. Note that the roasting cylinder is still surrounded by a brick oven and turned by steam.

French Gas Factory Roaster, Late Nineteenth Century

The new technology of gas began to appear in coffee roasting apparatus in the late decades of the nineteenth century. This French machine dumped the coffee by gravity from the bottom of the drum into the cooling tray.

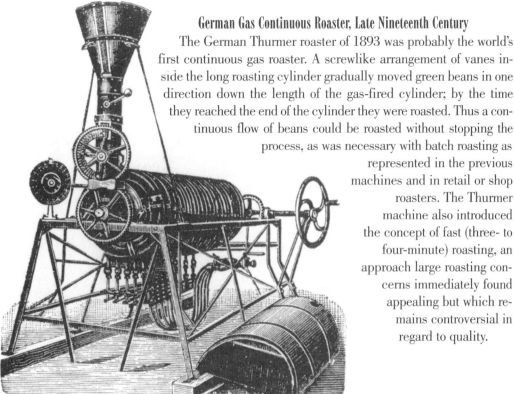

German Gas Continuous Roaster, Late Nineteenth Century

The German Thurmer roaster of 1893 was probably the world's first continuous gas roaster. A screwlike arrangement of vanes inside the long roasting cylinder gradually moved green beans in one direction down the length of the gas-fired cylinder; by the time they reached the end of the cylinder they were roasted. Thus a continuous flow of beans could be roasted without stopping the process, as was necessary with batch roasting as represented in the previous machines and in retail or shop roasters. The Thurmer machine also introduced the concept of fast (three- to four-minute) roasting, an approach large roasting concerns immediately found appealing but which remains controversial in regard to quality.

Cross-Section Continuous Roaster, Late Twentieth Century

Pictured here is a cross-section of a contemporary continuous roaster, looking down the interior of the drum. The roasting is accomplished by a powerful stream of hot air moving from one side of the drum to the other. The beans are cooled near the end of their ride down the cylinder by a combination of cool air and a fine spray of water.

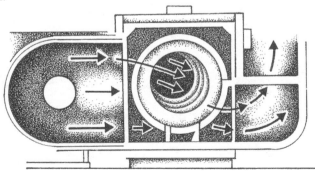

Large continuous roasters being installed today are increasingly likely to use the fluid-bed principle, however. They work much like oversized versions of the Sivetz shop roaster diagrammed on page 46. After one batch of beans finishes rotating and roasting in the stream of hot air, it drops into a cooling chamber and a fresh batch of beans replaces it, thus implementing continuous roasting.

From Cinnamon to Charcoal

Roast Styles

Nothing influences the taste of coffee more than roasting. The same green coffee can be roasted to taste grassy, baked, sour, bright and dry, full-bodied and mellow, rounded and bittersweet, charred. In appearance roasted beans can range from light brown with a dry surface through dark brown with an increasingly oily surface to black with an almost greasy look.

These differences in appearance lead people to talk about differences in roast *color*—from *light* roast to *dark*. I prefer the term *style* to describe the varying taste characteristics that roast imparts to coffee, since a coffee carried to a medium roast slowly, for example, will taste subtly different from the same coffee brought to the same medium roast quickly at higher temperatures. Others call the gradual change in color and taste created by roast *degree of roast* or *degree of processing*, which are accurate terms but clumsy. In this book I'll generally stick with the term *style*.

Changing Roast Traditions

Until recently preferences in roast style, like so many other cultural choices, were traditional. Style of coffee roast was a choice our particular time and place made for us. Thus Turks roast darker than Saudi Arabians; southern Italians roast darker than northern Italians; people in Normandy darker than people in central France. In the United States the Northwest has traditionally preferred a somewhat darker roast than New England, northern California darker than southern California, New Orleans darker than Atlanta.

These traditional preferences are the basis of many of the names used in the contemporary American coffee business to describe style

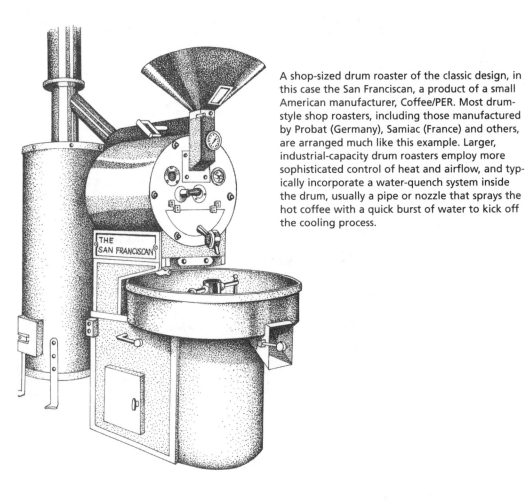

A shop-sized drum roaster of the classic design, in this case the San Franciscan, a product of a small American manufacturer, Coffee/PER. Most drum-style shop roasters, including those manufactured by Probat (Germany), Samiac (France) and others, are arranged much like this example. Larger, industrial-capacity drum roasters employ more sophisticated control of heat and airflow, and typically incorporate a water-quench system inside the drum, usually a pipe or nozzle that sprays the hot coffee with a quick burst of water to kick off the cooling process.

of roast: New England (light), American (medium), Viennese (slightly darker), French (still darker), Italian (still darker again), and so on. Names for roasts are discussed in more detail later in this chapter, and summarized along with other information on roast in a chart on pages 68–69. However, in our globally conscious, media-saturated times, regional uniformity in roast preference has begun to blur. Certainly in North American cities you can find virtually every possible style of roast sold by someone somewhere. The typical "American" roast style—medium brown in color, bright and dry in taste—now shares the shelves with darker roasts, and caffé lattes and cappuccinos are insinuating their foamy nuances into the culture of the bottomless cup.

What's Best?

Such cultural crossing and mixing makes it difficult to argue for any single "best" style of roast. One of the most frequent questions I'm asked when I'm identified as a coffee writer runs: What is the best coffee (best roast, best brewing method, best whatever) in northern California (in Seattle, in the world)? I understand that my questioners are simply trying to figure out how to start a reasonably interesting

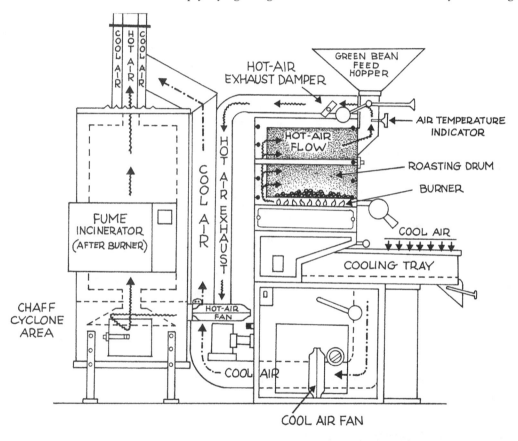

A cross-section view of the San Franciscan drum roaster pictured on the opposite page. The green beans are released from the cone-shaped hopper into the roasting drum. There they are roasted by a combination of heat applied to the outside of the drum and a flow of heated air drawn through the drum by the hot-air fan. A system of metal vanes (not shown) tumbles the beans inside the drum. When the beans achieve the desired roast a semicircular door is opened at the front of the drum enclosure, and the hot beans spill out onto the cooling tray. The cool-air fan then pulls room-temperature air down through the hot beans while paddles inside the cooling tray gently stir them.

After leaving the roasting drum, the hot air, now carrying roasting chaff and smoke, circulates in the chaff-cyclone area, dropping its chaff as it does so. The chaff-free hot air then continues upward through the fume incinerator or afterburner to be cleansed of its smoke and odors.

conversation with a coffee writer; nevertheless, such questions are impossible to answer. Comparing a dark-roast coffee to a medium-roast coffee is as pointless as comparing red wines to white. If some-one were to ask, "Which roaster, in your opinion, produces the best Italian-style coffee in northern California?" I could begin to think about responding. Even then I might ask the questioner whether she prefers a pungent, Neapolitan-style roast, good for drinking with hot milk, or a smoother, sweeter dark roast like those produced in north-ern Italy, good for drinking straight. Again, both styles of dark roast can be equally "good," depending on taste and expectations.

Of course people who sell coffee often have answers to such ques-tions: The "best" happens to be what they sell. Most roasters have clearly defined roasting and blending philosophies, arrived at after long experience. These dedicated professionals are certainly entitled to their positions, but to claim that a given approach to roasting is sci-entifically and objectively better than other approaches ultimately founders on the rocks of cultural difference. Who is to say to a French coffee drinker from Normandy who prefers a thin-bodied black coffee that tastes mildly burned that a coffee carefully brought to a medium roast is objectively and universally better than his because more of the flavor oils survive the roasting? Perhaps this French coffee drinker from Normandy prefers a charred taste to more flavor oils.

One of the many pleasures of home roasting is experimenting to determine what the "best" roasting style is *for you*. Of course one of the frustrations of home roasting is that once you get a batch of beans that taste exactly the way you want them to you may have trouble pre-cisely duplicating the procedure that produced them. But if you are at all systematic you can come very close to consistency, and home roasting is for romantics and adventurers anyhow. Those concerned purely with uniformity probably should stick to buying coffee from the store.

Bad by Any Standard

There are some clear parameters to good roasting, however, boundaries which, if transgressed, produce roasts that are bad by almost anyone's standard.

Look at the table on pages 68–69. In roasts that are too light, in which the internal temperature of the beans never rises above 390°F/200°C and the color remains a pale brown, the flavor oils stay undeveloped and the coffee will taste grassy, sour, and will be without aroma. In roasts that are too dark, in which the internal temperature of the beans has soared above 480°F/250°C and the color is definitively black, most of the flavor oils will have been burned out of the bean and the woody parts of the bean itself may be charred. Such coffee tastes thin-bodied, burned, and industrial.

Another way coffee can be roasted definitively badly is either by holding it too long at too low a temperature, which in roasting nomenclature is called "baking" the coffee, or by scorching the outer surfaces of the beans. Both mistakes are easy to commit for beginning home roasters, and need to be guarded against by carefully following the instructions on pages 146–172.

But so long as a roast avoids such extremes, only cultural preference and personal taste can determine which style is ultimately "best."

Names and Roast Styles

Currently used names for roast styles come from two sources. One is the general roasting preferences of various nations of coffee drinkers—Italian, French, and so on. The other grew up within the American coffee profession during the late nineteenth and early twentieth centuries. Both nomenclatures are necessarily vague, and are now being supplemented by a more objective numerical system based on instrument reading of color.

Geographical Roast Names

Let's take a quick run through the common roast names first, beginning with those that derive from coffee-drinking geography, since these are the names you are most likely to see on coffee bags and bins.

The lightest roast, *New England*, is hardly produced in North America anymore. The ordinary medium-brown roast that still dominates coffee taste in the United States is usually unnamed, but may be called *American*. A slightly darker roast, sometimes with tiny droplets of oil on the surface, may appear as *Viennese* or occasionally *light French*. *French* describes a moderately dark roast with more surface oil; *Italian* (sometimes *Spanish*, *Continental*, or *New Orleans*), darker and oilier still. A very dark brown, almost black roast, may be called *dark French* (since such a roast is favored in northwestern France), *Spanish*, *Turkish*, or *Neapolitan*. Lately a roast called *espresso* has been inserted between *French* and *Italian*, which roughly represents the current roast taste in northern Italy (moderately-dark brown with some oil on the surface of the bean).

Thus we get something that looks like this (sticking to the more popular terms):

- *New England* (light brown, dry surface)

- *American* (medium brown, dry surface)

- *Viennese* (medium dark brown, possibly flecks of oil on surface)

- *French* (moderately dark brown, light oil on surface)

- *Espresso* (dark brown, surface can range from very oily to barely slick, depending on roast procedure)

- *Italian* (dark, blackish brown, definite oily surface; most roasting establishments stop here)

- *Dark French* or *Spanish* (very dark brown, almost black, very oily).

Traditional American Roast Names

There is another naming system haunting the aisles of coffee stores, however, one based on traditional American roasting terminology stretching back to the nineteenth century. It breaks out about like this:

- *Cinnamon* (very light brown)

- *Light* (light end of the American norm)

- *Medium*

- *Medium high* (American norm)

- *City; high* (slightly darker than norm)

- *Full city* (definitely darker than norm; sometimes patches of oil on surface)

- *Dark* (dark brown, shiny surface; equivalent to *espresso* or *French*)

- *Heavy* (very dark brown, shiny surface; equivalent to *Italian*).

Of these terms *full city* is the only one used today with any frequency; roasters who bring most of their coffees to a style somewhat darker than the mid-twentieth-century American norm often describe their roast as *full city*.

Numbers to the Rescue: The Agtron/SCAA Roast Classification Color Disk System

Confusing? True. To help save the roasting world from arbitrary naming and obfuscation, the Specialty Coffee Association of America (SCAA) has recently released a kit for classifying roast based on precise machine reading of color.

The eight reference points in this classification system have no names, only numbers, and are matched with eight carefully prepared color disks. A sample of a roasted coffee, when finely ground and pressed into a petri dish, can be matched with a color disk, thus assigning it an approximate number on a scale variously termed a *chemistry index* or *Agtron gourmet scale*. These *color-disk* (or *color-tile*) numbers run from #95 (lightest roast) through #85 (next lightest) at intervals of ten down to #25 (darkest common roast).

Of course someone who owns an Agtron near-infrared spectrophotometer, an instrument that sells for between $15,000 and $20,000, can make very precise readings directly from the petri dishes of coffee.

At this writing the Agtron/SCAA system is so new that it is impossible to predict how it will enter the common language of roasting or show up on coffee signs and brochures. However, I have taken a stab at connecting the Agtron/SCAA classification-system numbers with common roast names in the comprehensive roast table on pages 68–69. Keep in mind, however, that the Agtron/SCAA system was designed without regard to the various traditions and preferences several generations of coffee roasters have attached to these names, and is intended to create a separate and hopefully more objective basis for discussion of roast.

The four color samples printed on the inside back cover give a rough idea of the range of the eight roast colors represented in the Agtron/SCAA system. Remember, however, that there are eight colors in the system, not four, and that the vagaries of color printing, the glossiness of the ink, the variability of light sources, the distractions of adjacent colors, not to mention what you had for lunch, all combine to make this abridged version of the Agtron/SCAA color disks technically useless. In other words, don't expect to be able to hold up a handful of beans next to these four color samples and be able to assign the beans an Agtron number. The samples will give you some general visual reference for the system as a whole, however.

For information on obtaining the Agtron/SCAA Roast Classification Color Disk System, plus information on the SCAA and Agtron generally, see Resources. Carl Staub, an innovative practical scientist and president of Agtron, is the principal researcher behind the color-classification system.

Tasting Terms

At no time does language seem so puny as when it attempts to describe how things taste. Nevertheless, coffee professionals *can* talk sensibly about the taste of their beverage. They do so by sharing common definitions of certain key terms and categories. Around these terms and categories subtler observations about taste can be arranged.

Here are a few of the most important terms for talking about differences in taste among green coffees and roast styles. I've left out technical terms that relate to specific phases of professional coffee-cupping, or taste evaluation, plus the seemingly endless list of words for defects in green coffees (*fermented*, *hidey*, *musty*, and so on), since these terms refer to problems that hardly apply to the fine coffees you are likely to buy from specialty stores or green-coffee dealers. Finally, I've disregarded popular terms that are self-evident or have no clear consensus meaning (*rich*, *floral*, *fruity*, *buttery*, and others).

The first three terms, *acidity*, *body*, and *aroma*, are relatively stable in meaning and almost universally used in coffee evaluation. Unless you understand them you can't properly talk coffee. The terms that follow those three are less likely to elicit consensus among tasters. They represent my selection from a large and growing list that includes traditional coffee terms dating back to the nineteenth century as well as new vocabulary being brought into coffee from wine and other tasting schemes.

Acidity, acidy. One of the most important tasting categories in coffee, and one of the most likely to be misunderstood. Neither acidic nor sour, an acidy coffee is brisk and bright. A good analogy is to the dry sensation in wines. Coffees lacking acidity tend to taste bland and lifeless. Some coffees carry their identity wrapped in their acidy notes. For example, coffees from Yemen and from East Africa (Kenya, Zimbabwe) display a striking, fruity, red-wine-like acidity. The darker a coffee is roasted, the less acidy it becomes. However, strong acidity in a green coffee may show up in a dark roast as sharpness or pungency.

Body, mouthfeel. Body is the sensation of heaviness in the mouth; it also registers as a rich, full feeling at the back of the palate. Body is a sensation, an element of taste, not a measurable fact. It can be confirmed by consensus among experienced tasters, but apparently has no direct correlation to the quantity of solids the coffee releases into the cup.

As coffee approaches a medium- to dark-brown roast, body *increases*. As it passes into a very dark roast (dark French or Spanish roast), body decreases.

Aroma. Although this term is self-evident in its general definition, it is important in discussions of roast. Aroma is less developed in very light roasts, peaks in intensity in medium to medium-dark roasts, and falls off in very dark roasts. For professional coffee evaluators or cuppers, some qualities of coffees may be more immediately apparent in the aroma than in the taste of the coffee itself. Certain green coffees produce more aroma than others, which often is taken as evidence of their power in the cup.

Complexity. Another obvious yet useful term. A complex coffee allows certain strong sensations such as acidity and sweetness to coexist. It presents a wide *range* of sensation, and often doesn't reveal itself immediately and definitively. Complexity is undoubtedly at its peak in the middle ranges of roast style, from medium through the moderately dark to dark roasts used for espresso. Yet a good espresso roast is complex in a different way from a medium roast, since the elements that compose that complexity subtly change. Most blends (those that aren't designed simply to save the blender money) aim to increase complexity.

Depth. Depth describes the resonance or sensual power *behind* the sensations that drive the taste of the coffee. It is a tricky and subjective term, but one that profitably invites us to consider how certain coffees open up and support their sensations with a sort of ringing, echoing power, whereas others simply present themselves to the palate before standing pat or fading.

Varietal distinction, varietal character. These terms seem to have migrated over to coffee from wine tasting relatively recently.

They describe qualities that distinguish one unblended green coffee from another when the coffees are brought to the relatively light "cupping" roast used in professional coffee evaluation. Examples are the powerful, winelike acidity and heavy body of Kenyan coffees, the ringing acidy notes and clean balance of Costa Rican, or the low-toned richness of Sumatran. Some coffees do not display pronounced varietal characteristics, which does not make them bad or boring. If they are particularly forceful yet balanced they might earn the epithet *classic*. Other good but not distinctive coffees may be praised as *good blenders* because they complement rather than compete with other, more unusual coffees.

Strictly speaking, terms like "varietal distinction" are misleading, since most coffees are not marketed by botanical variety but by *origin*. Thus the proper term should be "origin distinction" or "growing-region distinction." But those phrases are not half so impressive as "varietal distinction," with its oak-toned, wine-world panache.

Whatever we choose to call it, this quality displays itself best in light to medium roasts, becomes progressively more obscured in darker roasts, and is virtually impossible to detect in very dark roasts.

Balance.   Another self-evident term, this one describing coffees in which the acidity is strong but not overwhelming, the body substantial, and no taste idiosyncrasy dominates.

Wild, natural, earthy.   These are terms describing flavor notes that derive from some kinds of dry processing, in which coffees are dried with the fruit still attached to the bean (see Chapter 4). A slight sour twist to the acidity is the best verbal description I can produce. Once you identify this taste syndrome you'll know it forever. I enjoy wild-tasting coffees; they remind me that I'm drinking something that comes from the earth. But I'm a romantic. If this taste is too pronounced it becomes an outright defect.

Clean.   In some respects this term describes qualities that are the opposite of wild or natural. Clean-tasting coffees are free of defects, shadow undertones, or varietal distractions.

Roast-Related Terms

These are words specifically related to the overlay of taste that style or degree of roast contributes to green coffees.

Sweet. In medium-dark through moderately dark roasts (Viennese through espresso) the development of sugars combined with the partial elimination of certain bitter flavor components, like trigonelline, give the cup a rounded, soft taste and rich body without flatness. Some coffees come to a sweeter dark roast than others.

The term "sweet" also occasionally figures in discussions of the merits of green coffees brought to a lighter cupping roast. For example, some Peruvian or Mexican coffees may display a soft, mild quality a cupper may call "sweet."

Pungent, pungency. These words are my choice to describe the distinctive, bitterish twist that dark roasting contributes to taste. Any lover of dark roasts knows and honors this sensation.

Roast taste, bittersweet. Terms describing the characteristic collective flavor complex of darker roasts. The acidy notes are gone, replaced by pungent notes combined with a subtle, caramel sweetness. "Bittersweet" is my term; some people call this often unnamed group of sensations "roast taste" or the "taste of the roast."

Bready. A bready taste manifests in coffees that have not been roasted long enough or at a high enough temperature to bring out the flavor oils.

Baked. Another term for maltreated coffee. The coffee has been held too long in the roaster at too low a temperature; the taste in the cup is flat and without aroma.

Roast Styles and Flavor

Now let's look at how some of these key categories—acidity, body, aroma, varietal distinction, and bittersweetness or roast taste—transform as coffee is brought in stages from a very light to a very dark roast style. Again, this information is summarized for easy reference in the chart on pages 68–69.

- The most lightly roasted coffee (usually called *cinnamon*; internal bean temperature at conclusion of roast below 400°F/205°C; SCAA color tile #95) is very light brown in color, will display a strong, sometimes sour *acidity*, little *aroma*, an often grainy taste, and thin *body*. The surface of the bean will be dry.

- As the coffee achieves a more complete but still relatively light roast (*New England, light*; concluding internal bean temperature around 400°F/205°C; SCAA color tile #85), the *acidy* notes will be powerful, and the *varietal characteristics*, which often are nuances of acidity, will be pronounced. The *body* will be developed, but not as fully as it will become in a somewhat darker roast. The surface of the bean remains dry, as the flavor oils continue to develop in tiny pockets inside the bean.

- At a darker, moderately light to medium-brown roast (*light, medium,* unnamed, *American*; concluding internal bean temperature between 400°F/205°C and 415°F/215°C; SCAA color tiles #75 through #65), the *acidity* will be bright but less overpowering, the *varietal characteristics* still pronounced, and *body* fuller. For most traditional American East Coast coffee drinkers this style represents a "good" coffee taste.

- At a slightly darker, medium-brown roast (*medium, medium high,* unnamed, *American, city*; concluding internal bean temperature 415°F/215°C to 435°F/225°C; SCAA color tile #55), *acidity* remains strong though perhaps richer, *varietal characteristics* muted but still clear, and *body* still fuller. This is the traditional roasting norm for most of the American West.

- At a slightly darker roast than the traditional North American norm, one coffee professionals often call *full city* (concluding internal bean temperature 435°F/225°C to 445°F/230°C; between SCAA color tiles #55 and #45), *acidity* is slightly more muted and *body* slightly heavier. At this roast, only the more pronounced *varietal characteristics*, like the winelike acidity of

Kenya coffees, will persist. Subtler notes, like the elusive smokiness of some Guatemalan coffees, will be lost.

At this roast the first hints of an entirely new flavor appear: the taste taken on by darker roasts of coffee. This taste complex has no consensus name; in my list of tasting terms I call it *bittersweet*. Certain sugars are developed in the bean, giving it a subtle sweetness (*not* sugary, rather an understated caramel-like quality), while the acidity begins to transform into a pleasant pungency. The combination is familiar to any drinker of darker-roasted coffees.

The surface of the bean may remain dry, or oils may appear in tiny droplets or patches as they begin to rise from pockets inside the bean to its surface. This is the preferred roast style of many coffee drinkers in the American Northwest and northern California, and is currently being carried nationwide by the successful Starbucks chain.

- At a moderately darker roast (*espresso, European, high*; concluding internal bean temperature 445°F/230°C to 455°F/235°C; between SCAA color tiles #45 and #35), the *acidity* is largely folded into a general impression of richness, the *varietal characteristics* muted virtually beyond recognition, the *body* full, and the *bittersweet* notes characteristic of dark-roasted coffees rich and resonant. At this roast the surface of the bean always displays some oil, ranging from a few droplets to a shiny coating.

- When coffee is brought to a definitely dark roast (*French, Italian, dark*; concluding internal bean temperature 455°F/235°C to 465°F/240°C; SCAA color tile #35), the *bittersweet* or dark roast taste completely dominates, the *body* begins to thin again, and all remaining *varietal character* and *acidy* notes are transmuted inside the pungent richness of the dark roast flavor, which may range from rounded and mellow (in less acidy coffees) to bordering on bitter (in coffees that begin very acidy). The surface of the bean will be bright with oil.

- With very dark brown roasts (*Italian, dark French, Spanish, heavy*; concluding internal bean temperature 465°F/240°C to 475°F/245°C; between SCAA color tiles #35 and #25), the *body* continues to thin as more and more of the oils are evaporated by the roast, the bitterish side of the *bittersweet* equation becomes more dominant, and a slight charred taste may appear. Needless to say, *acidy* notes and *varietal characteristics* have long since been transformed into nuances of the dark-roast flavor. The bean is shiny with flavor oils driven to the surface.

Despite the somewhat thinner body and dominance of the dark roast flavor, such a coffee can be a bracing and pleasant experience for those who like it. It can be particularly pleasant drunk with hot milk as a caffè latte or similar espresso-and-milk drink.

- The ultimate dark roast, almost black (*dark French, Spanish*; concluding internal bean temperature 475°F/245°C to 480°F/250°C; SCAA color tile #25) is definitely a special taste. The *body* is even thinner, the *bittersweetness* is still more bitter and less sweet, and burned or charred notes dominate. At this roast all coffees, regardless of origin, tend to taste about the same. The surface of the bean is glossy with oil. This unusual roast is not an espresso roast, by the way; espresso is best brewed with one of the dark-but-not-black, fuller-bodied, sweeter roasts described earlier. Home roasters typically have an opportunity to sample this ultimate dark roast, since sooner or later we all produce a batch whether we plan to or not.

- Beyond this point the coffee is definitively burned: it has no body, tastes like charred rubber, the oils are driven off the surface of the bean, and the roast is worthless.

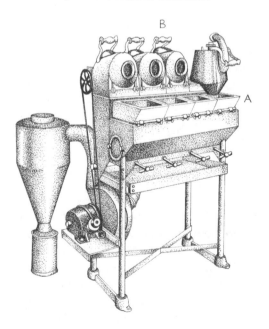

Sample roasters are used to prepare small quantities of green coffee for purposes of evaluation. Most are miniature drum roasters arranged in a battery, like this set dating from the early twentieth century. The roasted beans are dumped into the cooling trays (A) at the front of the drums by lifting the handles (B) at the back. The drum on the right is in the forward, dumping position. Heat is usually provided by gas, as it is here. An electric motor drives the drums, and a fan (here enclosed in a circular housing under the drums) sucks hot air through the drums, evacuating both roasting smoke and chaff. The chaff settles to the bottom of the cyclone at the rear of the machine. The fan also helps cool the beans by pulling fresh air down through perforations in the bottoms of the cooling trays.

Time/Temperature Ratio and Other Subtleties

All roast styles differ in taste depending on *how* the roast is achieved. Coffee brought to a given roast color quickly—by higher roast temperature or a combination of higher temperature and rapidly moving air currents—will usually preserve more acidy notes than will coffee brought to the same degree of roast at lower air temperatures over a longer period of time. On the other hand, a slower-roasted coffee tends to be fuller in body and more complex in taste.

These differences in approach are the source of often bitter controversy among proponents of various roasting systems. In particular, an intense behind-the-scenes struggle for the hearts and minds of newcomers to the coffee-roasting world is being carried on between what I like to call the slow-and-deliberate school of roasters versus the fast-but-gentle camp.

The slow-and-deliberate school likes to bring the coffee along in careful, methodical stages: first at relatively lower temperatures to force out free moisture from the bean, then at somewhat higher temperatures once the chemical transformation of pyrolysis has kicked in. The goal is to preserve as much as possible of the bean's original moisture and cellular structure during the roast process by using temperatures just high enough to maintain the forward momentum of the roast, yet low enough to minimize damage to the cellular matrix of the bean and its bound moisture. The slow-and-deliberate camp tends to prefer drum roasters to fluid-bed equipment, because drum roasters typically permit a finer and more precise control over roast temperatures and air velocity than do fluid-bed roasters. Roast times for the slow-and-deliberate faction usually range in the twelve- to twenty-five-minute range.

On the other hand, the fast-but-gentle roasters argue that the longer the beans are in the roaster the more aromatic oils they lose. Consequently, they are usually proponents of fluid-bed systems, or those systems in which a column of hot air simultaneously agitates and roasts the beans. The fast schoolers contend that the high velocity of the roasting air in fluid-bed machines transfers heat to the beans so efficiently that you can bring a coffee along quickly without drying it out excessively or destroying its cellular structure, thereby preserving the maximum amount of its flavor components. Roast times among the fast-but-gentle contingent may be as short as five minutes, usually no more than fifteen.

Who's right?

Perhaps both are. The controversy may simply hinge on what you ultimately consider "good" coffee.

If you favor a bright, acidy cup (or a sharp, pungent cup in dark roasts) with a clean, straightforward flavor profile, you may weigh in as backer of the fast-but-gentle school.

On the other hand, if you prefer a fuller, less acidy cup, emphasizing complexity and depth rather than assertive brightness (or rounded sweetness rather than sharp pungency in a dark roast), you may back the slow-and-deliberate platform.

Both camps acknowledge that coffee held at too low a temperature for too long a time will taste baked and flat, while coffee brought to a given roast style too quickly at too high a temperature will lack complexity, resonance, and power.

Thus both sides aim for quality; it simply may be that they nuance quality in different ways.

The nature of the roasting technology also influences the taste of a given roast. Proponents of fluid-bed roasting, for example, argue that their roasts taste better and cleaner because the roasting smoke and chaff are blown off the beans more decisively than is the case with most drum roasters. Other professionals may *like* the somewhat heavier, oilier taste imparted by smoke and burning chaff, and may deliberately stick with older roasting equipment that allows some of the smoke to work around the beans.

Time/Temperature Ratios and the Home Roaster

The foregoing nuances are best ignored by all but the most advanced of home roasters. Your first task is to learn how to control the timing of the roast so that you get the broadly defined roast style or color you prefer.

Your ability to experiment with subtler taste differences related to the *way* you achieve a given roast style depends above all on the equipment you use.

I propose four technologies for home roasters in this book: (1) stovetop crank corn poppers; (2) hot-air corn poppers and similar fluid-bed roasting devices; (3) gas ovens; and (4) electric convection ovens. Each tends to produce a roast emphasizing certain taste characteristics.

Those who like a bright, acidy coffee are probably best served by a fluid-bed roasting technology as represented in hot-air corn poppers and comparable home roasters. The temperature in the roasting chamber is usually fixed in these devices. They produce a relatively rapid roast (seven to twelve minutes), and the roasting smoke is effectively blown off the beans, all promoting a clean, high-toned flavor profile.

Those who prefer a more idiosyncratic roast taste with heavier body and a fuller profile may be best off with an old-fashioned stove-top corn popper that achieves a given roast more slowly and allows the roasting smoke to work around the beans. If you install the recommended thermometer in your popper you can exert some control over roast temperature, permitting you to roughly accentuate certain taste characteristics through a faster roast and others through a slow.

Coffees prepared in gas ovens often display a striking complexity and depth of flavor because the irregularity of the roast coaxes a wider range of taste out of the coffee than do methods that produce a more regular, uniform roast. The relatively long roast times in gas ovens also promote a rather full body and relatively rounded, low-acid flavor profile. Like the modified stove-top corn popper, gas ovens permit some limited control of time/temperature ratios and hence roast nuance.

Finally, there are electric convection ovens. The extremely long, slow roast produced by these appliances creates a clean-tasting, full-bodied, but *very* low-acid cup. Coffees roasted in electric convection ovens will taste dull to most palates, although some may enjoy their gentle, understated sweetness.

For more practical information on these possibilities see Chapter 5 and the roasting instructions on pages 150–172.

Green Coffee Characteristics and Roast Style

The moisture content and hardness of green coffee beans affect how quickly they roast and how they respond to various roast temperatures. The moister and denser the bean the somewhat more slowly it will roast and/or the higher the temperature needs to be in the roast chamber. More technically inclined roasters precisely measure the density and/or moisture content of the bean and modify their roasting procedure accordingly.

Such exact accommodations are not an option for most home roasters. However, there are a few rules of thumb based on the age of a green coffee and how it has been handled that can be usefully followed at home . These are included in the home-roasting overview in Chapter 5 and the practical instructions on pages 150–172.

Quick Reference Guide to Roast Styles

Most of what you really need to know about roast styles can be determined from the following chart. Extended explanation of terminology and categories can be found in Chapter 3. The roast colors associated with the tile numbers in column four are represented (roughly) on the flap inside

Roast color	Bean surface	Approximate bean temperature at termination of roast	Agtron Gourmet scale numbers; SCAA color tile number in bold face (see pages 55–56)	Common names
Very light brown	Dry	Around 380°F/ 195°C **"First crack"**	95 - 90 **Tile #95**	**Cinnamon**
Light brown	Dry	Below 400°F/205°C	90 - 80 **Tile #85**	**Cinnamon** New England
Moderately light brown	Dry	Around 400°F/ 205°C	80 - 70 **Tile #75**	**Light** New England
Light-medium brown	Dry	Between 400°F/205°C and 415°F/215°C	70 - 60 **Tile #65**	**Light Medium American** Regular Brown
Medium brown	Dry	Between 415°F/ 215°C and 435°F/ 225°C **"Second crack"**	60 - 50 **Tile #55**	**Medium Medium-high American** Regular City
Medium-dark brown	Dry to tiny droplets or faint patches of oil	Between 435°F/225°C and 445°F/230°C	50 - 45 **Tile #45**	**Viennese Full City Light French Espresso** Light espresso Continental After dinner
Moderately dark brown	Faint oily patches to entirely shiny surface	Between 445°F/230°C and 455°F/235°C	45 - 40	**Espresso** French European High Continental
Dark brown	Shiny surface	Between 455°F/ 235°C and 465°F/ 240°C	40 - 35 **Tile #35**	**French Espresso** Italian Dark Turkish
Very dark brown	Very shiny surface	Between 465°F/240°C and 475°F/245°C	35 - 30	**Italian Dark French** Neapolitan Spanish Heavy
Very dark (nearly black) brown	Shiny surface	Between 475°F/245°C and 480°F/250°C	30 - 25 **Tile #25**	**Dark French** Neapolitan Spanish

the back cover. The commonest of the common roast names listed in the fifth column are bold-faced. The stars under the tasting categories indicate the following judgments:

- • characteristic is weak, thin, negligible.
- •• characteristic is moderately clear, discernible.
- ••• characteristic is clear, full, substantial.
- •••• characteristic is at its peak.

Acidity	Body	Aroma	Complexity	Depth	Varietal Distinction	Sweetness	Pungency	Comments
•••	•	••	••	•	••	•		Roasts at the extreme light end of the roast spectrum can taste sour and grainy. Used only for inexpensive commercial blends.
•••	•	••	••	•	••	•		
••••	••	•••	•••	••	••••	•		
•••	•••	•••	••••	•••	••••	••		The traditional norm for the eastern United States.
•••	•••	••••	••••	••••	•••	••	•	The norm for most of the western United States.
••	••••	••••	•••	••••	••	•••	••	The norm for northern California and the Northwest.
•	••••	•••	•••	••••	•	••••	•••	The norm for northern Italy and North-Italian style espresso cuisine.
	•••	••	••	•••		•••	••••	The norm for most American espresso cuisine. Slight burned undertones appear.
	••	••	••	••		••	•••	Burned tones become more distinct.
	•	•	•	•		•	••	Burned or charcoal-like tones dominate.. Not a typical roast in the United States.

What to Roast

Choosing Green Beans

*E*very green coffee holds in its vegetable heart a slightly different collection of secrets. One of the pleasures of roasting at home is becoming acquainted with those intimacies in a far more direct and active way than by simply tasting someone else's roasted coffees.

Of course you may not care about the subtle differences among beans, only the general result: cheaper and fresher coffee. If so, you might simply buy a few pounds of green Colombia, Kenya, or Sumatra, skip to pages 150–172, and start roasting. Suggestions for obtaining green coffee beans and roasting paraphernalia can be found in Resources.

Eventually, however, you may want to begin exploring the full range of taste distinctions among the world's fine coffees. You can explore a single great coffee in a variety of roast styles, for example. Or you can develop a sort of cellar of green coffees from which you can choose at your own and your guests' whims. Finally, you can experiment with composing personal blends in a far more thoroughgoing way than you can by relying on the already roasted coffees of others.

Green Coffee Basics

The world's coffees are many and their differences complex. What follows is a general orientation to selecting green coffees from the point of view of the home roaster. Very serious aficionados may want to seek out a copy of Philippe Jobin's *The Coffees Produced Throughout the World.* See Resources for specialized books on coffee.

Keep in mind that the ultimate test of a coffee is not its name, or its grade, or any of the rest of the muttering that we attach to things,

An illustration from Jean La Roque's *Voyage de l'Arabie Heureuse (Voyage to Arabia Felix),* 1716. Coffee trees of the arabica varieties grown in Yemen, or historical Arabia Felix, do have a sparse, sturdy look like this one. Other arabica varieties may tend toward a fuller, droopier profile.

but rather its *taste*. If you try it and like it, then it's a good coffee. And if you don't like it, then you should be prepared to ignore all of the pontificating that tries to convince you otherwise.

Narrowing the Field: Species and Market Category

Given the bewildering variety of the world's coffees, it is probably just as well that we can dismiss some categories at the outset.

First, our considerations can be narrowed on the basis of *species*. Botanists now recognize approximately one hundred species of coffee plant, but only one, *Coffea arabica*, is the source of all of the world's most celebrated coffees.

The coffee species second in importance in world coffee trade is *Coffea robusta*, or *Coffea canephora*, as it is known to botanists.

1 Fruit du Café
dans sa maturité

3 Fruit Sec   2   1   4

4 Noyau, appelle
graine, ou feve du Café

2 Coupe du meme Fruit

Robusta grows at lower altitudes than *arabica* and is more disease resistant. *Robustas,* as coffees from the robusta tree are called commercially, generally lack the acidity and complexity of the best arabica coffees, although they often display a satisfyingly heavy body. They are used mainly as unnamed constituents of the cheaper coffee blends that line the aisles of supermarkets and fill the carafes of cost-conscious restaurants and corporate lunchrooms. Their only importance in the world of fine coffees occurs in relation to espresso. Small quantities of better-quality robustas are sometimes used to give body and sweetness to espresso blends.

A second candidate for dismissal is coffee from arabica trees grown at relatively low altitudes in Brazil. Known in the trade as *Brazils,* these coffees are stripped from the trees rather than selectively picked and handled carelessly. Together with robustas they contribute the preponderance of the coffees used in packaged preground and soluble coffee blends. Similar low-quality arabicas grown in countries other than Brazil are sometimes called *hard* coffees. They compete with Brazils in price.

Other, better coffees are also grown in Brazil. These, together with all of the other better arabica coffees of the world, fall into the third great market classification, variously called *milds* or *high-grown milds*.

It is the many coffees making up this third category that we turn to now. These are the fancy coffees of the world, which appear in the bins and bags of specialty coffee stores, and these are what you will be buying and roasting.

The Tortuous Question of Coffee Names

Before launching into a quick circumnavigation of the world of mild or fancy coffees, a word (actually quite a few words) about coffee names is in order.

Fancy or specialty coffees are sold in two forms: *blends,* mixtures of coffees from more than one crop or region, and *unblended* coffees from a single crop and region (often called *straight* or *varietal* coffees). Unblended coffees are of most interest to home roasters because they facilitate knowledge (you know what you're roasting), adventure (they often taste intriguingly different), and control (once you get a feel for various individual coffees you can begin to assemble your own blends).

Most unblended or straight coffees are labeled on the lists of exporters and importers by *country of origin,* by *market name,* and by *grade.* Grade often includes references to *processing methods* and occasionally to *growing conditions*, like altitude. An increasing number of coffees may be identified also (or alternatively) by the name of the *estate* or *cooperative* where they were grown and (occasionally) by their *botanical variety*. Let's look at each of these naming categories in order.

Country of Origin

This designator (Kenya, Colombia, and so on) is easy to understand. It is the one descriptive term that always appears on store labels and coffee bags. However, countries are large, coffees in any given country are many, and market forces complex. Hence the various names and categories that follow.

Mysterious Market Names

A market name is a traditional identifier that appears on burlap coffee bags and on exporters' and importers' lists. Most market names originated in the nineteenth century or even earlier. They derive from a variety of sources. Most refer to region (Guatemalan *Antigua* or Mexican *Oaxaca*), a few to a port through which the coffee is traditionally shipped (Brazilian *Santos*) or even to a port through which the coffee once was shipped but isn't anymore (Yemen *Mocha*; Mocha is a now closed and forgotten port on the Red Sea).

However, market names ultimately describe a coffee, not a place. Market names carry specific associations that include not only growing regions, but certain taste characteristics. Some market names are more famous than the country of origin. Hawaiian Kona coffee is typically known by its market name, Kona, not by its country of origin, United States, or even by its state of origin, Hawaii.

Layers of Grade Names

Coffee is also sold by grade (Kenyan AA, Colombian Supremo, and so on). Grade names can be based on evaluative criteria ranging from how big the bean is to how high the coffee is grown, to how good it tastes (cup quality). Grading criteria are usually established by coffee bureaucracies in the growing nations in an effort to discipline growers and encourage quality. Grading also provides a framework for sellers and buyers to describe and negotiate their transactions. In

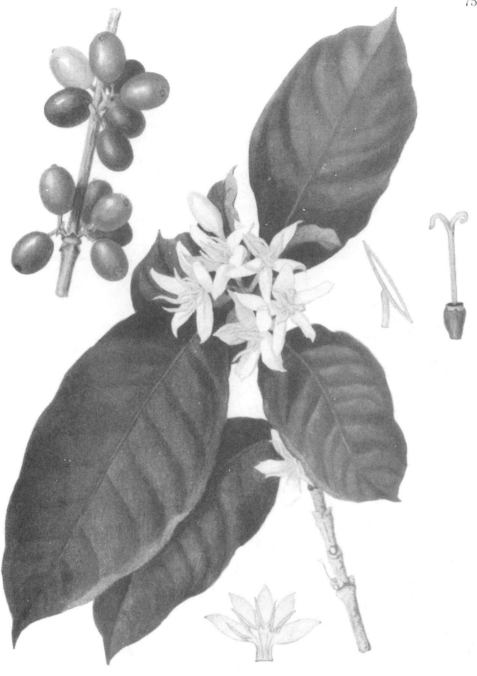

This illustration hints at the beauty of coffee trees in flower: The white blossoms with their delicate, jas-minelike abandon contrast strikingly with the shiny, dark-green leaves.

general, the grading process tends to focus more on externals, like how many sticks or defective beans a coffee harbors, than on subjective criteria like taste.

Bulking coffee in large generic lots according to grade traditionally has been a way for coffee bureaucracies of growing countries to maintain centralized control over the coffee enterprise. However, as more and more growing countries join the current global trend toward deregulation and allow individual growers and grower associations to cut their own deals with buyers, the importance of grading for the fancy-coffee business may be waning. In one growing country after another, the discipline of regulation as embodied in grading standards

Selective picking is crucial to quality coffee, since ripe and unripe fruit typically inhabit the same branches, and the unripe will spoil the ripe if both are allowed to co-mingle after picking. Machines that literally vibrate the ripe fruit off the tree are now in use in some parts of the world, but most coffee still is picked by skillful workers like this woman, whose hands deftly move down the branches, plucking the ripe fruit and allowing it to drop into the basket at her waist.

is being replaced or supplemented by the discipline of the market as embodied in competition among individual growers and grower associations for the attention of roasters and buyers in consuming countries.

Nevertheless, grade names remain an important element of coffee nomenclature. The more informative coffee store may identify a coffee by country (Guatemala), by market name (Antigua), and finally by grade (strictly hard bean). As a rule, however, stores qualify the country name of a bulk coffee with only one adjective, either grade or market name.

One particularly confusing grading term that often appears in importer and store literature is *peaberry*. The peaberry (*caracolillo* in Spanish) is a single round bean that sometimes appears inside the coffee fruit in place of the usual two beans. Peaberries may be mixed in with the normal beans, or separated and sold as a distinct grade of a given coffee.

Peaberries generally are considered to embody the characteristics of any given coffee with somewhat greater intensity than normal beans from the same crop. Although this judgment is based on the rather folkloric-sounding argument that peaberries contain in a single bean all of the good things normally contained in two, many reliable professionals confirm the notion on the basis of informal experiment.

For home roasters peaberries present a special advantage: they tend to roast more uniformly owing to their regular shape. In particular, roasters who use a stove-top corn popper will find that the rounded shape of peaberries make them easier to agitate than normal beans with their motion-resistant flat side.

The Wet and the Dry: Processing Method and Grade Names

The coffee bean is actually a seed of a small fruit coffee people call a *cherry*. How the fruit is removed from the bean and how the bean is dried are steps collectively known as processing. Since processing is one of the most important influences on coffee quality and taste it is no wonder that names for various processing methods figure so largely in grading and other descriptions of green coffees.

In the *wet method* the various layers of skin and fruit around the bean are stripped off gently and gradually, layer by layer, before the bean is dried. Such *wet-processed* or *washed* coffees tend to be more consistent, cleaner, and brighter, or more acidy, in taste than *dry-*

processed, natural, or *unwashed* coffees, which are dried with the coffee fruit still adhering to the bean. The dried fruit is subsequently removed from the dry beans, customarily by machine. Dry-processed coffees are generally more idiosyncratic in flavor and heavier in body than wet-processed coffees.

Semiwashed coffees are a sort of compromise. The skin of the cherry is removed immediately after picking, but the flesh or pulp is allowed to dry on the bean. The dried pulp is later stripped off by a machine that temporarily wets the bean again. Some have argued that semiwashed coffees felicitously combine the full body and complexity of dry-processed coffees with the clarity and acidity obtained by the wet method. The great coffees of Sumatra are usually semiwashed coffees, and coffee estates in Brazil are beginning to utilize the process with apparently impressive results.

Understanding the basic differences among wet, dry, and semiwashed processes is crucial to informed coffee connoisseurship. See pages 80–81 for an illustrated review.

How coffees are dried also may affect flavor and quality. As a rule, *sun-dried* coffees are considered preferable to machine-dried coffees, although here again various compromises and combinations and nuances complicate the picture. Beans may be partly dried by the sun and partly by machine. Coffees dried by machine at somewhat lower temperatures are more desirable than those dried at higher temperatures. Handling during drying is also important. Sun-dried coffees that have been protected from nighttime moisture during drying may be favored over sun-dried coffees that have been left unprotected at night, for example.

Growing Conditions and Grade Names

Finally, the altitude at which coffee is grown figures in many grade names. Arabica coffee beans grown at higher altitudes typically mature more slowly than beans grown at lower altitudes, and the resulting denser bean may display more acidity and sometimes more complexity in the cup. As with most coffee generalizations, however, this one entertains many exceptions. Certainly growing altitude is only one aspect of many that influence coffee quality and flavor. In Mexico, the Caribbean, and Central America it figures in various grade names, ranging from the explicit *high-grown* to the less explicit *altura* (height or altitude), a grading term in Mexico, and *strictly hard bean,* a name for the highest grades of coffee in Guatemala and Costa Rica (the higher the altitude the denser or "harder" the bean).

Turning to environmental issues, some coffees are *shade-grown,* with the smallish, pruned coffee trees interplanted among other trees and crops like bananas, whereas others are *sun-grown,* cultivated in dense, regular rows open to the sun. Environmentalists support shade-grown coffees because the canopy of trees creates an environment that shelters migrating birds and other wildlife and reduces erosion and dependence on chemical fertilizers. The shade-versus-sun distinction does not figure in traditional grading descriptions, but it often does appear in promotional literature. The issue is most relevant in regard to Central American coffees, since these have been traditionally shade-grown, and historically have provided key shelter for migrating birds. Yemen coffees, the most traditional coffees in the world, have always been grown in full sun, as have most coffees in Brazil and many other parts of the world.

Organic is an important descriptive term in the contemporary coffee world. An organically grown coffee must be certified by an international agency as having been grown without synthetic chemical fertilizers, pesticides, or herbicides. Somewhat lower yields and the considerable cost of the certification process account for the higher prices demanded for many organic coffees.

Estate and Cooperative Names

As the specialty coffee trade matures, closer relationships are being established between individual growers and buyers. These direct relationships mean that a specific coffee often no longer needs to be combined or "bulked" with other coffees from the same region in large lots to reach roasters and their customers.

Owners of quality-conscious coffee farms enlist the aid of their colleagues in consumer countries to establish *estate identities* for their coffees. Estates also may be called *fincas* (in Spanish-speaking Latin America), *plantations,* or simply *farms.* These estates, fincas, or farms may be large establishments that remove the fruit from the bean and dry the coffee at their own facilities, or occasionally smaller enterprises that process their coffee through cooperatively run facilities, but maintain control of their product. In either case, estates sell their coffees directly to dealers without mixing them with other coffees from the same region, in theory insuring that these coffees reflect consistent growing conditions and processing practices.

A similar consistency is achieved by some cooperatives of smaller growers that market their coffees separately like estates through special arrangements with coffee dealers or roasting establishments. These designated cooperative coffees often support environmental and/or social agendas.

Confusion and chicanery have developed around the estate concept, just as they have around other areas of coffee marketing. The

---

STAGES OF WET-PROCESSING COFFEE

The various steps in removing the skin and fruit from the coffee bean or seed are collectively called processing. Here, in cross-section, are the main stages of *wet processing*, the most common and also the most elaborate method of processing used for fancy coffee.

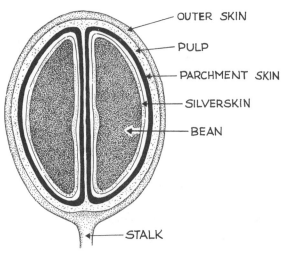

OUTER SKIN
PULP
PARCHMENT SKIN
SILVERSKIN
BEAN
STALK

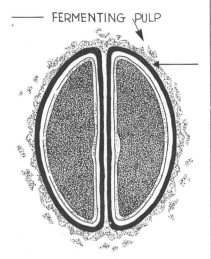

FERMENTING PULP

1. Ripe coffee fruit
The coffee fruit is protected by pulp and several layers of skin. In wet processing, these layers are removed one by one.

2. Pulping and fermentation
The first stage of processing is called *pulping*. Immediately after the beans are picked the outer skin of the fruit is slipped off by machine, exposing the sweet, sticky pulp. The pulp is then removed by fermentation: The fruit is held in open tanks, permitting enzymes and then bacteria naturally present in the fruit to literally consume much of the pulp from the beans. The remainder of the pulp is easily washed away.

STAGES OF WET-PROCESSING COFFEE (continued)

3. Drying in parchment
The beans, now separated
and pulp-free but still in
their parchment and silverskin, are dried, usually in
the sun on open terraces,
but sometimes in machines.
At this point the coffee is
said to be *in parchment.*

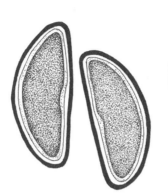
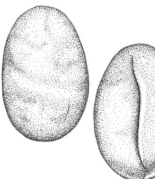

4. Hulling
Finally the parchment and
silverskin, both now dry
and brittle, are crumbled
off the beans by machine,
a stage called *hulling.* Fragments of the silverskin still
adhere to the bean, how-
ever. These tiny, paperlike
flakes float away from the
beans during roasting, con-
stituting the often trouble-
some *chaff.* In some cases
the grower removes the
chaff by subjecting the coffee to a last tumbling
called *polishing.*

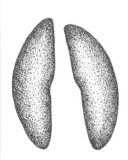

OTHER PROCESSING METHODS

Dry method. In this process the entire fruit is dried immediately after picking. The shriveled skins
and pulp are then abraded from the beans in a single final step.

Semiwashed method. As in the wet method, the outer skin is first removed by machine. But the
middle step in the wet method, fermentation, is skipped. Instead the beans are dried with pulp,
parchment, and silverskin all still attached. These three layers are removed in a last step, usually
involving wetting the beans and scrubbing them in specially designed machines.

Processing influences both flavor and appearance. Wet-processed coffees are regular in
appearance and typically display clean, consistent taste and aroma and bright acidity. Dry-processed
and semiwashed coffees may have more broken beans, and may exhibit more idiosyncratic, heavier-
bodied, often more complex flavor profiles because the beans were dried while in contact with the
fruit.

sheer number of growers currently scrambling to cash in on the estate idea creates confusion. Some estates may depend more on hype than on quality. Others may coast on a reputation that their coffees no longer merit. In one case a roaster was caught selling another, cheaper coffee in place of a very expensive estate coffee, the celebrated Wallenford Estate Jamaican Blue Mountain.

Most estate coffees do not command the extraordinary prices of the Wallenford Estate coffee, however, so they are less liable to promote deceit. Furthermore, the better-established estate coffees are handled by dealers and roasters who have too much pride and reputation at stake to play games with their customers.

Some Good Things About Estate Coffees

What are the advantages and disadvantages for home roasters of pursuing estate (and designated cooperative) coffees?

Advantage number one: The estate concept helps identify coffees in precise terms. If you buy the same coffee a second time it most likely will display the same characteristics that attracted you to it in the first place. Coffees sold by regional market name (as Guatemalan Huehuetenango or Mexican Coatepec) may come from farms miles apart, for example, and those sold by country and grade (Colombian Excelso, Peruvian AAA) may have been grown hundreds of miles apart.

A second advantage to buying by estate is that you can select coffees according to specific growing practices, social practices, or processing techniques. Many estates and cooperatives now specialize in organic coffees, for example. Other cooperatives support social agendas aimed at improving the lives of the farmers who grow the coffee and empowering them socially and politically. Some estates may specialize in a certain kind of processing technique or certain botanical varieties of *Coffea arabica*.

A third advantage to estate coffees is that many offer superior or distinctive versions of regional taste characteristics. For example, the well-known La Minita estate coffee of Costa Rica represents an intensification of all of the qualities that have made Costa Rican coffee admired: intense acidity; full body; clear, bell-like balance. On the other hand, some estate coffees may offer surprises. I recently tasted an estate coffee from the Shevaroy Hills district of India called Cauvery Peak that simply breaks the mold of most Indian coffees. To the low-key, heavy-bodied profile typical of Indian arabica coffees it adds a dominating, spicy acidity.

Some Less-Than-Good Things About Estate Coffees

Disadvantages to buying coffee by estate or cooperative?

Above all, if you become too concerned with buying only estate coffees you're limiting yourself. There are many outstanding coffees that simply are not marketed by estate. A reliable source—dealer, roaster, or store—that tastes coffees carefully before purchase may offer coffees that are identified only generically by market name, yet are as good as or better than similar estate coffees with their four-color brochures and marketing push.

A second disadvantage: price. Estate coffees may be good or different, but they may not be good or different *enough* to warrant the considerably higher price often asked for them. And some, unfortunately, may not be much better than ordinary coffees from the same region. In these cases the estate owners may have put more effort into publicity than into quality.

Finally, some estate and designated cooperative coffees may be difficult to find green. Estates and cooperatives tend to work through a few selected wholesale roasters or dealers, sometimes only one, so access to these coffees is often limited.

Old Versus New: Names for Botanical Variety

All fine coffees derive from the arabica species, but not all coffees derive from the same botanical *variety* of that species. Consider the differences among apples: Golden Delicious and McIntosh, for example; or wine grapes: Cabernet Sauvignon and Pinot Noir, Sauvignon Blanc and Chardonnay. There is little doubt that botanical variety is one of the main influences (along with climate, soil, altitude, and processing) on the taste characteristics of coffee. (An aside: botanists often distinguish between *cultivars* or cultivated varieties of a species and naturally occurring varieties, or between varieties and *strains,* groups of individuals within a variety that share common characteristics. Coffee professionals who are not botanists generally apply the term *variety* to all three: variety, cultivar, and strain. I use the term with similar expedient inclusiveness here.)

The fine-coffee world is only beginning to market coffee by variety (or cultivar or strain). At most we may learn that an estate's coffee trees are Bourbon and Typica, or Caturra and Catuai. More often we have no idea whatsoever which arabica varieties produced the fruit that produced the coffee we are drinking.

Despite (or perhaps because of) the fuzzy communication around variety, it is a great and intensifying source of conflict in the coffee world. The connoisseurs and traditionalists raise the banner of what they call *old arabica* varieties, while some scientists, coffee growers, and government officials defend the usefulness of *new arabicas*.

In fact, the old varieties often are not that old. But they are spontaneous. Nature itself with its inscrutable processes caused these mutants to appear suddenly on someone's coffee farm at some point in the past, and human intervention was confined merely to taking advantage of that gift by preserving its seed through selection. Some of the most famous of traditional arabica varieties are the Mocha of Ethiopia and Yemen; Typica and Bourbon, which until recently dominated the coffee fields of Latin America; the Blue Mountain of the Caribbean; Sumatra from Indonesia; and Kent, which originated in India and has been widely planted in East Africa. The most striking of these spontaneous mutants is Maragogipe, a variety with very large beans (but low yields per tree) that appeared in about 1870 in Brazil. Mundo Novo also turned up in Brazil, but rather late in the game, about 1920. Caturra is another relative newcomer (1935), but has been planted widely in Latin America because of its compact growth and high yield.

New arabica varieties, as you can guess, are those that have been developed deliberately through crossbreeding programs. Colombia, Brazil, and Kenya have been particularly successful in developing new disease-resistant or higher-bearing varieties, sometimes based on complicated interspecies crosses between varieties of arabica and robusta. The controversy is taste: Many coffee buyers claim that these concocted varieties may pay off for the farmer by producing more coffee at less risk of crop loss, but only at the cost of cup quality. Officials of government agencies responsible for the crossbreeding programs tend to disagree, of course, arguing that the economic benefits of the new varieties outweigh any slight loss on the drinking end of things. New arabica varieties have been accused of reducing the cup quality of some Colombian coffees, and the sinister-sounding new variety Ruiru 11 has admirers of Kenyan coffees nervous about the future of what has been one of the most dependable and abundant of the world's great coffees.

As the world of fine coffee grows more sophisticated, botanical variety doubtless will figure more prominently in identifying and marketing coffees, and aficionados may be in a position to make their own assessment of the impact of botany on quality.

The Ultimate Challenge: Adding Roast Names

Keep in mind that style of roast also can figure in the names that appear on store labels and signs. Most straight, unblended coffees are offered in a "normal" American medium to moderately dark roast, in which case the roast style is not named. However, if an unblended coffee is offered in a style darker than normal, the name of the coffee and the roast style both may appear: Sumatran Mandheling Dark Roast, for example. Thus, theoretically it might be possible to see a coffee designated Costa Rican (country) Tarrazú (market name) La Minita (estate) Washed (process) Strictly Hard Bean (grade) French Roast, although such lengthy and informative labeling is seldom seen for fear customers may nod off before buying the coffee, thus reducing sales. Furthermore, most dark-roast coffees sold today are blends, although occasionally you may see popular coffees like Colombia or Sumatra offered in a dark-roast style.

Circumnavigating the Coffee Globe

To make the most of the quick tour around the coffee globe that follows, make sure you understand the key tasting terms defined in Chapter 3 (pages 58–60), particularly *acidity* (the dry, bright sensation produced by a coffee brought to a medium roast), *body* (the sense of thickness and richness imparted by a coffee), and *varietal distinction* (the principal taste characteristics that distinguish one coffee from another at a light to medium roast).

Classic Coffees: Latin America and Hawaii. At their best, the classic coffees of Latin America and Hawaii manifest full body, bright acidity, and a clean, straightforward taste. They provide what for a North American is a normative good coffee experience.

The most admired of these coffees are balanced yet powerful: strong in all respects, from the rich vibrancy of the acidity through their full body and complex flavor. As a rule they are grown at high altitudes, although climatic conditions like cloud cover and consistent moisture can mimic the effect of higher altitudes and produce a similar flavor profile.

Other classic coffees may be grown at lower altitudes or in conditions that encourage a softer, sweeter taste, with a lighter, brisker acidity, rather than the powerful, vibrant acidity of the "bigger" classic coffees.

Preceding page: An assortment of marks of the kind that appear on coffee bags, which ultimately are the origin of many of the terms used in importers' lists and coffee-store signs and brochures. The majority of the marks in this illustration, from the early twentieth century, are Colombian. Typically they display the name or initials of the exporter, the market name (Medellín, Armenia), and the grade name (Excelso). There are also marks from Sumatra (market name Mandheling), from Ethiopia (Djimah, Longberry Harrar), Venezuela (Mérida), and several from Brazil (Santos). In two cases the marks refer to botanical variety: the desirable "bourbons" or beans produced by trees of the bourbon variety.

The classic Latin American/Hawaiian taste is based in part on the brightness and clarity of flavor achieved through wet processing. Almost all fine Latin American and Hawaiian coffees are washed, the exceptions being the better dry-processed and semiwashed coffees of Brazil.

Buying the Classic Coffees. Quality coffees in the classic mode are produced in many regions of Mexico and Central America, the Caribbean, and South America, as well as in Hawaii. The most consistently celebrated coffees probably come from the highlands of Guatemala (market names, Antigua, Cobán, and Huehuetenango) and Costa Rica (Tarrazú, Tres Ríos), from Colombia, and from the Kona district of Hawaii. Jamaican Blue Mountain is a famous coffee, but an expensive and rather controversial one. Mainly on the basis of my own assessment, I would add Puerto Rican Yauco Selecto to a list of particularly distinguished or celebrated classic coffees.

The Big Classics. Generally fine Costa Rican, Guatemalan, and Colombian coffees are "big" coffees: full-bodied, with a bracing, rich acidity. They are best enjoyed at a medium to medium-dark roast, so that the power and subtle nuances of their acidity can be enjoyed.

The best Guatemalan coffees generally display a bit more intrigue and complexity than their Costa Rican counterparts, which are known for their powerful, bell-like clarity. This difference may be owing to botanical variety; most Costa Rican coffee derives from the newer Caturra variety of the arabica species, while Guatemalans for the most part appear to have stuck with the traditional Typica and Bourbon cultivars.

At one time Colombian coffee was remarkably consistent, but in recent years it has slipped, and the difference between one estate or supplier's Colombia and another's may be marked. The best Colombian coffee tends to come from beans of the older Bourbon and Typica varieties rather than from Caturra or the more recently developed hybrid cultivars like Colombiana. Some estates or exporters may specify botanical variety in their promotional literature. The highest grade of Colombian coffee, Supremo, is usually somewhat better than the next grade down, Excelso, even though the grading is done on the basis of bean size and appearance. Coffee with a more specific market or estate designation tends to be better than the generic MAM (Medellín-Armenia-Manizales), a designation that in effect covers a good part of the mountains of west-central Colombia.

The Caribbean Classics. The finest Caribbean coffees (best coffees of Puerto Rico, Jamaica, the Dominican Republic, and coastal Venezuela) are also powerful, but generally lower-toned, with their acidity held inside a deep, sweet, long-finishing richness.

True Jamaican Blue Mountain coffee, like the original Wallenford Estate Blue Mountain, is a big, rounded, intense, yet perfectly balanced example of the classic Caribbean taste. Whether you are willing to pay prices for it that are triple to quadruple what you would pay for a fine Guatemalan or Costa Rican coffee is up to you. There are also somewhat lower-grown, softer, smaller Jamaican coffees (grade designations, *Blue Mountain Valley, High Mountain Supreme, Prime Jamaica Washed*) that are good coffees but should not demand the extraordinary prices asked for the true Blue Mountain. Do not pay high prices for coffees labeled "Jamaican Blue Mountain Style" or "Jamaican Blue Mountain Blend," by the way. The former will have no Blue Mountain in it whatsoever, and the latter may have very little.

A combination of relatively high labor costs and high local consumption turned Puerto Rico from a coffee exporter to an importer during recent decades. In the last few years, however, an estate selling its coffee under the traditional market name Yauco Selecto is attempting almost single-handedly to revive the tradition of fine export coffee on the island of Puerto Rico. Yauco Selecto is pricy. However, the samples I've tried suggest it is a superb coffee in the best Caribbean style: complete, classic, with substantial body, rich acidity, and a low-toned, complex flavor profile. In fact, it reminds me very much of the fine Wallenford Estate Blue Mountain coffees I recall tasting twenty years ago when I researched my first book on coffee. And remember that with Puerto Rican as well as Hawaiian coffees a substantial part of the price premium goes to support a relatively higher standard of living for workers than prevails in most coffee-growing regions of the world.

I also recently tasted some excellent Caribbean-style coffees from the Dominican Republic (often marketed as Santo Domingo) and coastal Venezuela. Haitian coffee tends to be a particularly low-toned, sweet version of the Caribbean mode.

The Gentle Classics. Good Brazilian, Peruvian, Panama, and Mexican coffees generally are lively rather than overpowering in acidity, lighter in body than the bigger classic coffees, and rounded in flavor. They make excellent darker roasts for espresso drinks. Their gentler acidity also makes them attractive coffees for those who like to drink their coffee black and unsweetened.

Other Central and South American coffees less often seen—from Nicaragua, Ecuador, and El Salvador—also are typically softer, "smaller" versions of the classic taste.

The Hawaiian Classics. In the big picture Hawaiian coffees may be somewhat overpriced and perhaps a bit overpublicized. However, the best estate Hawaiian Kona is a powerful, rich, acidy example of the classic taste, though perhaps softer than the best high-grown Guatemalan and Costa Rican origins. Lesser grades of Kona sold generically will be good but not exceptional, and the same warning regarding "style" and "blend" given earlier in regard to Jamaican coffees applies to Kona. Premium coffees from the other Hawaiian islands have not been on the market long enough to establish clear identities, although the growers appear inspired and serious in their pursuit of quality.

One of the great advantages of Hawaiian coffee for the aficionado is its accessibility. Growers are beginning to lavish the same attention on Hawaiian coffee as vintners did a couple of decades ago on California wines. It has become relatively easy to visit the farms, and proprietors increasingly provide plentiful and detailed information on their coffees, including botanical varieties and processing details. But remember, the ultimate proof is in the cup, not in the design of the four-color brochure.

Classic Coffees with a Conscience. The close relationship between many Latin American and Hawaiian growers and North American buyers has led to the development of various programs and niche coffees that attempt to blunt the destruction that a relentlessly price-driven agricultural commodity like coffee tends to wreak on the earth and people of the growing regions.

In effect, these programs ask the consumer to pay a bit more for a coffee to support social and/or environmental agendas.

For those interested in ecological issues, for example, there are several certified organic cooperative coffees from Peru, Mexico, and Central America. Estate-grown organic coffees are produced in Costa Rica, Guatemala, Hawaii, and an increasing number of other locations. If you are not concerned about organics but still wish to support progressive social and economic agendas, Haiti, Costa Rica, and Guatemala all market coffees produced by associations of small-grower cooperatives. Or you can purchase your coffee from one of many roasters and chains that publicize their contributions to Coffee Kids, an organization that directs contributions toward programs that support small growers. To reach Coffee Kids directly, see the contact information list in Resources. Finally, several estates publicize their equitable and supportive treatment of their staff and workers, while others promote their commitment to shade-grown coffees.

How much variety and quality does a home roaster give up by buying only organic coffees, or only coffees from farms and cooperatives that pursue conspicuously sustainable agricultural practices and/or progressive social agendas?

Clearly, home roasters who buy only environmentally or socially correct coffees are limiting their options. The idea of marketing coffees in terms of social programs or growing conditions (organic, sustainable, shade-grown, and so on) is largely restricted to Hawaii and Latin America, where close relationships have been worked out between growers and continental North American dealers. For example, most Ethiopian coffees are probably grown without chemical fertilizers, herbicides, or pesticides simply because farmers can't afford these products. But dealers seldom know for certain what goes on with these coffees, so they clearly can't be *labeled* as organic.

How good are environmentally and socially correct coffees? Overall, this is an unanswerable question, although the coffee business is full of people with opinions about how it should be answered.

A coffee's flavor is only as good as *all* of the many factors that influence flavor make it: botanical variety, soil and altitude, age and condition of the trees, and picking, processing, and storage methods. An organic or progressive coffee could be superior in all of these categories, in which case it will be a splendid coffee, or inferior in all of them, in which case it will be a dud. Exactly the same can be said of any coffee, including those that are conventionally grown. Organic or sustainable agricultural processes taken by themselves indicate nothing one way or the other about the cup quality of a coffee, nor, obviously, do the social programs pursued by the grower.

Ultimately, you need to taste the coffee and make your own assessment. See Resources for suggestions on obtaining green coffees that respond to various environmental and social concerns. I offer a more detailed discussion of issues centering on these coffees in my *Coffee: A Guide to Buying, Brewing & Enjoying.*

Romance Coffees I: East Africa and Yemen

The coffees of Africa, Asia, and the Malay Archipelago (Indonesia and Papua New Guinea) provide an array of romantic alternatives to the classic coffees of Latin America and Hawaii.

East Africa, together with Yemen, just across the Red Sea from Africa, produces some of the most distinctive of the world's coffees. Most are characterized by an extraordinary winelike acidity, which can range from rough and wild in dry-processed Ethiopian coffees (Harar, Jimma), to rich and robust in Kenyan, to earthy and subtle in Yemen Mocha coffees. Similar winelike notes enliven excellent arabica coffees from Zimbabwe and Uganda.

However, some washed or wet-processed coffees from Tanzania, Malawi, and from Ethiopia (those sold under the market names Yirgacheffe and Limu in particular) are soft, full, rounded, and floral.

Probably the best place for home roasters to begin in their exploration of East African coffees is Kenya. The state-of-the-art Kenyan coffee industry produces a plentiful yet superb product that is relatively easy to obtain green. Despite a recent fall-off in quality owing to the introduction of new hybrids, Kenya remains a big, powerful example of the East African taste: almost overpowering in its burgundylike acidity, full-bodied and provocative. That last term may be a cute fashion-industry word, but it's a good word for Kenyan coffee. Brewed strong, Kenya will *provoke* a response; it makes you notice that you're drinking coffee—a good coffee and a striking one.

Ethiopia, the original home of *Coffea arabica*, produces the most varied range of coffee taste experience of any country—or indeed any region—in the world.

After sampling a Kenya, I would try an Ethiopian Harar to experience the wildness and roughness of the dry-processed Harar taste. Harar is not considered a great coffee, but like Kenya it is a surprising coffee, with its high-toned, fruity wildness. Unlike Kenya, however, it is usually a lighter-bodied coffee and its acidity is much rougher.

Ethiopian Yirgacheffe is perhaps the world's most remarkable coffee. It is full-bodied, soft, and rich, but its most striking characteristic is its extraordinary floral perfumes. The intense fruit or wine notes of most East African coffees here become evanescent and flowerlike. Other southern Ethiopian washed or wet-processed coffees (Limu and Washed Sidamo) offer somewhat less distinctive versions of the Yirgacheffe taste profile.

The next coffee from this part of the world to try (if you can find

one) is a good Yemen Mocha. Mocha, like Ethiopian Harar, is a traditional dry-processed coffee. With Mocha the dried fruit is removed
from the beans by hand, using the most simple and ancient of methods. The shriveled husk of fruit is broken open with a simple mortar
and pestle, and the crushed fragments of the fruit husk are separated
from the beans by tossing or pouring both through the air and fanning
or blowing on them, sending the lighter fragments of husk floating
away from the heavier beans.

Owing to this traditional approach to processing, Yemen Mocha
arrives at the roaster with a good many broken beans and pebbles. But
if this unprepossessing-looking coffee is a true Mocha, it will display
a particularly rich version of the winelike acidity of Africa and Arabia, heavier in body than the Ethiopian Harar, deeper and richer-
toned, yet still vibrant with fruitlike resonances.

When a dealer buys a Yemen Mocha it often may not be clear
whether the coffee in question has been grown entirely in Yemen, or
whether along the line someone hasn't mixed in some dry-processed
beans from Ethiopia or Kenya. The signs of a true Mocha are the richness of its acidity and its substantial body. But even suspect Mochas
can be exciting coffees. A final complication to the Mocha story:
Some dry-processed Ethiopian coffees also carry the traditional market name Mocha, so if you run into a coffee identified only by that
name inquire as to its origin.

Clearly identified estate coffees from some parts of East Africa
are difficult to turn up. The lack of direct contact between North
American importers and African growers means the growers have difficulty establishing a clear, marketable identity in the United States,
and in some cases regulation in the growing countries designed to
control prices, support small growers, and assure consistency and
quality discourages growers from cutting special deals with exporters
and importers. Nevertheless, many outstanding East African coffees
are available in the United States.

A last note of clarification: There are many variant spellings in
English of Ethiopian and Yemeni names. Mocha may also appear as
Moca, Mocca, or Moka; Harar as Harer, Harrar, or Harari; Jimma as
Djimah or Jima; Gimbi as Ghimbi; Yirgacheffe as Yrgacheffe.

Romance Coffees II: India, Indonesia, New Guinea

Coffees of the arabica species grown in a crescent stretching from southwestern India across the Indian Ocean through Sumatra, Sulawesi, and Java to New Guinea offer another kind of romance: the intrigue of softness, richness, and heavy, resonant body. These qualities reach their peak in the best coffees of Sumatra and Sulawesi (old name Celebes), which wrap a deep-toned acidity inside their extraordinarily rich body.

The better coffees of Java and Papua New Guinea offer similar, though perhaps less distinctive, experiences. Coffees from southwestern India tend to be the least arresting of the group. They often lack sufficient acidity to enliven the body, and may taste heavy rather than rich. They are excellent blending coffees, however, and one importer has been bringing estate versions into North America that brighten the typical low-key Indian taste profile with a light-toned, spicy acidity.

Processing Asian-Pacific Coffees. There may be a wider variation in processing method in the India-Indonesia-New Guinea crescent than anywhere else in the world.

Coffees in India are processed by both wet and dry methods. And to complicate the picture, some dry-processed coffees are also *monsooned,* a process whereby coffees are deliberately exposed to moisture-bearing winds (see pages 94–96).

Coffees in New Guinea and Java are generally wet-processed. Coffees from Sumatra are most often semiwashed, but may be dry-processed or wet-processed. Some are dried over wood fires rather than by sun or machine. Such regional variations in processing may contribute to the full body and idiosyncratic taste of many Indonesian coffees.

Indonesia is also the principal source of exotic (and scarce) *aged* coffees (see pages 94–96).

Buying Asian-Pacific Coffees. Where to start? Undoubtedly with a good Sumatran coffee.

After having been the private pleasure of aficionados for years, the great coffees of Sumatra have been discovered by a larger clientele and have risen in price. New Sumatran coffees have entered the market that are largely inferior to the traditional origins. Nevertheless, it is possible to find good Sumatran coffee (generally marked Mandheling or Lintong) at a reasonable figure.

Much quality Sulawesi coffee goes to Japan, but as a rule you can find estate coffees, usually with the regional name Toraja or Kalossi appearing somewhere in the description.

The Java arabica coffee industry was wiped out by the leaf-rust disease in the late nineteenth century and replaced by plantings of robusta, but the Indonesian government has helped revive the tradition of fine arabica coffee in Java. These revival Java coffees are marketed as Java Estate or Java Estate Arabica. Unlike most Sumatran coffees they are wet-processed, which may account for their somewhat lighter body and less complex flavor. Nevertheless, they retain the rich tones typical of Indonesian coffees.

Papua New Guinea coffees are also excellent representatives of the deep-toned, rich Asian-Pacific taste. The best of these wet-processed coffees can be extraordinary: subtle, smooth, with a sort of echoingly resonant full body.

Indian coffees, as I indicated earlier, tend to be low-key, sweet versions of the great Indonesian coffees, full-bodied but without the acidity and complexity of the Indonesian origins. Some coffee drinkers may prefer their gentleness. Coffees from the Shevaroys and Nilgiris districts may be more acidy and brighter.

Recently an estate coffee from Australia has come onto the North American market. The sample I cupped was rather underpowered, without sufficient acidity to give its good body complexity or interest.

Romance Coffees III: Aged and Monsooned Coffees

Aged and monsooned coffees constitute another exotic possibility for the home roaster.

If green coffee is stored correctly, it maintains its flavor rather well. As it ages, acidity slowly decreases and body increases. Thus a given coffee drunk as *new crop* (first year after harvest) generally will taste brighter, with slightly more acidity and less body, than the same coffee consumed as *past* or *old crop* (a year or more past picking and processing). Some dry-processed coffees are deliberately held and sold as old crop because their slight grassiness or other defects mute or transform with time.

Aged (also called *vintage*) coffees carry the taste transformation wrought by time to its extreme. Some aged coffees have been held for as long as ten or more years before being exported or roasted, although three years is probably the norm. A true aged coffee has overwhelmingly heavy body, yet preserves just enough acidity to shimmer in its depths and add intrigue to its heaviness. Eventually, aged coffees begin to lose all acidy notes and turn dull and syrupy rather than rich. Even these coffees can be a pleasant change of pace drunk straight, however, and a delight in blends.

Why are some older coffees considered aged, whereas others are patronized as simply old? Why do some three-year-old coffees taste deep, rich, and vibrant (aged), while others taste flat and dull (merely old)? The only comprehensive answer I turned up was from a man who pointed out that if an older coffee tastes good we call it aged, whereas if it tastes bad we call it old.

It appears that the great aged coffees of Indonesia are stored in the usual burlap sacks in warm, rather humid conditions, but well ventilated and out of direct rain or sun, and periodically rotated to even out exposure to moisture. I suspect further revelations in regard to proper aging of coffees will come to light as the specific traditions associated with the fine aged Indonesian coffees become better documented.

A taste profile somewhat similar to aged coffees is achieved in considerably less time by Indian exporters who "monsoon" their coffee. This exotic process involves holding the coffee in special warehouses open to the moist monsoon winds. In a few weeks the coffee yellows and transforms in taste. The samples of monsooned coffee I have cupped are not nearly as rich and resonant as fine aged coffees, but share a certain heaviness on the palate, together with an odd, interesting chocolaty or caroblike finish. They are cleaner in taste than aged coffees, which may make them more attractive to some.

Both aged and monsooned coffees are special tastes. The fondness for them among Europeans probably derives from the Java coffees brought to Europe in the eighteenth and nineteenth centuries in the holds of sailing ships. In the moist darkness of the long passage these coffees sweated and transformed in flavor much as monsooned coffees do.

The tradition of such coffees in Europe doubtless accounts for the fact that most aged or specially handled coffees come out of India or Indonesia, regions that provided most of northwestern Europe's coffee during the eighteenth century. You may occasionally see aged African or Latin-American coffees for sale, however.

At any rate, you may want to try an aged and a monsooned coffee, first straight in order to understand their taste, then perhaps in a blend, where the weight and body of specially handled coffees can be used as a resonant counterpoint to brighter origins.

Buying Aged and Monsooned Coffees. Currently the most widely available specially handled coffee is Indian monsooned Malabar, a source for which can be turned up in most cities with a few phone calls and some persistence. For the rarer (and more expensive) aged coffees you probably need to resort to mail order, if they can be found at all. Aging coffee involves a long-term commitment that fewer and fewer exporters are willing to make. Some of the suppliers listed in Resources may be able to turn up a good aged coffee for you.

Home roasters, of course, have the option of pursuing their own experiments with aging coffee. See pages 104–106.

Blends and Blending

Coffee blends are crafted for two reasons: (1) to save money; (2) to produce a coffee that tastes better than (or at least different from) coffees of a single crop or region.

For large commercial roasters the cost issue is paramount. Since their coffees compete in supermarket chains, mass-market blenders attempt to create a decent coffee as cheaply as possible. Bland but acceptable "price" coffees (robustas and/or the inexpensive low-grown, mass-processed arabicas called *Brazils*) are combined with smaller quantities of more expensive, more acidy and flavorful coffees from the high-grown milds category. Blenders who work for large coffee-roasting concerns must be extraordinarily skillful, since they need to create a blend that tastes the same month after month from constituent coffees that constantly change as prices and availability shift.

Specialty-coffee roasters who sell smaller quantities of coffee in whole-bean form to a more demanding clientele also may want to cut costs by blending. But the primary goal of most specialty roasters is to produce a blend that tastes better or more balanced than any of its constituent coffees. Rather than the one or two blends offered by commercial supermarket roasters, specialty roasters may offer as many as ten or twenty. These blends may differ according to roast style (a blend for Viennese roast and one for Italian, for example) or embody subtle taste variations within a single style (medium-roast blends ranging from brisk and light-bodied through heavy-bodied and rich, or espresso blends extending from rounded and sweet to rugged and pungent).

Other blends aim either to mimic characteristics of a famous and expensive coffee (Jamaican Blue Mountain Style Blend), or stretch a costly coffee by mixing it with similar but cheaper beans (Hawaiian Kona Blend).

The final kind of blending is done by customers of specialty-coffee stores themselves, who may craft their own blends on the spot from the assortment of already roasted coffees offered at their favorite coffee source. Some particularly caring coffee-store proprietors may even prepare personalized blends on an ongoing basis for their regular customers.

Blends and Home Roasting

Home roasters can, like their commercial counterparts, pursue blending for cost reasons, taste reasons, or both. Before pursuing either alternative in detail, it might be well to discuss the general theory of blending.

Blending can be a very subtle procedure. Some roasters blend new crop and old crop beans of the same coffee to obtain a fuller, more balanced version of that particular coffee's taste than could be obtained by roasting either new or old crop beans alone. In this case the goal is to make a certain coffee taste more like itself, to fulfill its inner potential, as it were.

In other situations the goal may be to create an entirely new taste that never existed before. For example, the world's oldest and most famous blend, Mocha-Java, combines one-third acidy Yemen Mocha with two-thirds deep-toned Java coffee. The Yemen Mocha enlivens the Java while the Java balances and enriches the Mocha. A new taste is created.

In still other circumstances the goal may be to produce a coffee appropriate to certain culturally defined tastes. Italians in Milan like a subtle, sweet, yet lively espresso. Italians in San Francisco's North Beach prefer a rougher, more bitter or pungent style. Although North Beach espressos are roasted darker than Milan espressos, the blend of constituent beans is different as well. Most North Beach espresso blends combine rich, acidy coffees with a base of softer Mexican or Brazilian coffees. Most Milan blends are mainly arabicas with soft profiles, like Brazilian Santos, combined with high-quality robustas for sweetness and body, but with no sharp, acidy coffees whatsoever. In these cases the definition of good coffee in the respective cultures determines the goal of the blending project.

Yet, no matter what the goal of blending, the fundamental approach is the same: combining complements, or putting together coffees that fill in weaknesses without obscuring strengths.

Blending at Home: Getting Started

For home roasters, subtlety in blending may only be possible after considerable tasting and experimentation. It is probably easier to get a feel for the process by combining very different but complementary coffees; a bright, acidy coffee with a fuller, deeper-toned coffee, for example.

To help that process along, here are lists of some well-known coffees divided into categories according to the particular qualities they might contribute to a blend. Obviously there are numerous ways of categorizing coffees for blending purposes; my lists offer only one approach to a complex subject. Also keep in mind that there are many nuances and exceptions to the generalizations around which these categories are built.

Category 1: Big classic coffees. These coffees contribute body, powerful acidity, and classic flavor and aroma to a blend. They perhaps make too strong a statement for use as a base for blends, but are excellent for strengthening and energizing less acidy coffees with softer profiles.

Guatemala (Antigua, Cobán, and Huehuetenango, other good
    Guatemalan coffees)
Costa Rica (Tarrazú, Tres Ríos, other good Costa Rican coffees)
Colombia
Venezuelan Táchira, Mérida

Category 2: Smaller classic coffees. These are "good blenders"; they establish a solid, unobtrusive base for a blend, and contribute body and acidity without competing with more individualistic coffees. When brought to a darker roast, they often confer a satisfying sweetness. I've omitted more expensive coffees like Jamaican Blue Mountain, Hawaiian Kona, and Puerto Rican Yauco Selecto, which given their cost probably should be enjoyed straight.

Mexico (Oaxaca, Coatepec, Chiapas, Tapachula)
Dominican Republic (Baní or Cibao Altura for more acidity;
    other origins for less)
Peru (Chanchamayo for more acidity; Northerns for less)
Brazilian Santos (washed for more acidity; dry-processed or
    semiwashed for more body and sweetness)
Panama Boquete
Coastal Venezuela (Caracas, Caripe)

Other possibilities are the better coffees from El Salvador,
Ecuador, Nicaragua, and Haiti.

Category 3: East African and Yemen coffees. Their powerful winelike acidity makes these coffees a poor base for a blend, but
excellent contributors of complexity and liveliness. Some, like Kenya,
contribute considerable body as well. These coffees should be used
with care in blends for darker roasts; they add a sharp bite attractive
to many (including me), but may be distracting to others.

Yemen Mocha (adds richness and body as well as acidity)
Kenya (ditto above; acidity even more powerful)
Zimbabwe
Ugandan Bugishu
Ethiopian Harar (contributes rough, fruity, exciting acidity, but
less body than the preceding)
Malawi

Category 4: Asian-Pacific and similar coffees. These add
richness and body to a blend, and combine well with other coffees.
Their deep-toned acidity will anchor and add resonance to the lighter,
brisker coffees of Category 2, and balance without blunting coffees in
Categories 1 and 3.

Sumatra (Mandheling and Lintong for more character and body;
other origins for less)
Sulawesi (Toraja, Kalossi)
Java arabica
New Guinea
Ethiopian washed coffees (best are Yirgacheffe and Limu)
India (best estate coffees from Nilgiris and Shevaroys contribute
liveliness and acidity; other origins tend to add weight with-
out much power)

Category 5: Aged and specially handled coffees. These
add weight and body to a blend, and in the case of aged coffees richness and complexity as well. They are fun to experiment with in
blends as a balance to Category 1 and 3 coffees.

Any good aged coffee
Indian monsooned Malabar

Blending to Save Money

If you are a home roaster blending mainly to save money you first need to invest in one or more full-size 120- to 150-pound bags of green coffee. Maximum savings from home roasting can be realized only by buying green coffee in bulk.

One approach might be to buy a bag of good quality but reasonably priced coffee from Categories 1, 2, or 4, then add complexity by blending it with smaller amounts of other coffees purchased as you go along. People who like a big, classic taste might make the base for their blends a Colombia; those who like a lighter, softer classic taste might make it a Mexico or Brazil. A Sumatra makes a good base for blending, but will cost a bit more per pound than a Colombia or Mexico. Of course, before committing to 130 pounds of a single coffee you should live with it first. Buy a couple of pounds green, roast it to the style you prefer, and drink it for a few days. If it provides what seems to you a good fundamental coffee taste, go back to the supplier from whom you obtained the sample and try to arrange to buy an entire bag, or see Resources for advice on buying green coffee in bulk.

Next experiment with adding smaller quantities of other coffees based on the categories noted earlier. The additional coffees might be those designed to add acidity and body (Kenya), or richness and body (Sumatra or Sulawesi), or heaviness (an aged coffee).

Blending for Taste and Variety

Clearly there are two ways to approach blending for taste alone: by system and by improvisation.

One systematic approach would be to start with a base coffee, as I suggest in the previous section, roast and drink it long enough to really *know* it, then experiment with adding other coffees to it, keeping notes as you go along. Another approach might be to begin with two coffees that complement one another, like the acidy Mocha and the softer, fuller Java of the original Mocha-Java blend (I'd make them a Kenya and a Sumatra), experiment with the proportions of the two constituents until you learn how they work together, then begin experimenting with adding a third coffee, again keeping notes so that a success can be built upon or duplicated.

If you intend to line up your blends and cup them against one another in professional fashion, you should probably use a hot-air corn popper or similar fluid-bed roaster (see pages 154–161), since these devices permit you to roast a series of small samples rapidly and consistently.

Obviously blending by improvisation needs no instruction. Buy coffees from two or three of the categories I noted above and combine them as moment and mood suggests. It is probably still a good idea, however, to use one or two familiar coffees as a consistent base for your caprice.

Blending for Espresso and Dark Roasts

When blending for espresso cuisine the first question to consider is how you and your guests take your espresso. If you tend to drink it without milk and with very little sugar, you probably should avoid the big, acidy coffees in Categories 1 and 3 and rely mainly on coffees in Categories 2 and 4. Italian blenders prefer a base of Brazilian Santos, whereas West Coast Americans typically rely on Mexican and Peruvian coffees. Good Indonesian coffees make splendid dark roasts, but are relatively expensive. Some Italians like to use high-quality robustas to smooth out their espresso blends.

On the other hand, if you drink your espresso with a good deal of hot milk and/or sugar, you may prefer a more pungent blend. On a base of Brazil, Peru, or Mexico, try adding a coffee from Categories 1 or 3, perhaps either a Costa Rica or a Kenya or some of both. Go easy at first, adding a little more of the big, acidy coffee every session, until you achieve a taste you like for the way *you* drink your coffee. If you know you like an assertive, twisty espresso, start with a base of Kenya and gradually soften it with increasing amounts of a gentler coffee.

Of course how dark you roast your espresso blend and what method you use to roast it also profoundly affects flavor. See Chapters 3 and 5.

Roasting for Blends

The components of a blend can be roasted separately and then blended, or blended and later roasted. The roast first, blend later approach undoubtedly produces a more interesting and complex flavor profile, particularly if the components of the blend are brought to slightly different roast styles. But roast first, blend later is a lengthy process, since to assemble one blend you may have to roast as many as four or five separate batches of beans. So don't hang your head if you take the easy way out and combine all the coffees of the blend into a single batch before roasting them.

Blends of Roasts

When I first came into coffee consciousness in the San Francisco Bay Area twenty years ago, blends of dark- and medium-roasted beans were common. They are less so today, which is probably a pity. For me one of the most vibrant and exciting ways to enjoy a coffee is to mix darker and lighter roasted beans of the same origin, thus experiencing the coffee in its full range of roast taste.

Try it. Take the same coffee and bring two batches to a medium and to a dark or moderately dark roast, then blend the two. If you enjoy the result, try varying the identity of the two coffees. Blunt the acidity of a Kenya by carrying it to a moderately dark roast, then combine one part of the darker-roasted Kenya with two parts of a medium-roasted Indonesian coffee, for example.

A Note on Decaffeinated Coffees

Coffees are decaffeinated in their green state. Three principal processes are used today in the world of fancy or specialty coffees: the *traditional* or *European process*, the *water-only* or *Swiss-Water process*, and the *CO^2-water* or *Sparkling-Water process*. All are consistently successful in removing all but a trace (2 to 3 percent) of the resident caffeine.

The traditional and water-only processes follow roughly the same steps: (1) The beans are soaked in hot water until both flavor agents and caffeine have been soaked out of them; (2) they are removed from the water, and the caffeine is removed *from the hot water*, leaving the flavor agents behind in the water; (3) the beans are then recombined with the water, where they reabsorb the now caffeine-free flavor agents. Once dried, the beans are ready for sale and roasting.

In the water-only process the caffeine is removed from the hot water by means of activated charcoal filters. In the traditional or European process the caffeine is removed by means of a solvent, usually ethyl acetate. The solvent selectively unites with the caffeine, floats to the surface of the hot water, and both caffeine and solvent are skimmed off the surface, leaving only the flavor agents behind.

The water-only approach is attractive to consumers because it uses no chemicals. The traditional or European process has fallen out of favor because of the sinister notion that a *solvent* is involved in the procedure. Reassurances that (1) the solvent never touches the coffee itself; (2) the most widely used solvent, ethyl acetate, has not been implicated in health or environmental issues; and (3) the solvent is so volatile that any trace that persists through the process is doubtless burned off during roasting, together constitute too complex a response for most coffee drinkers. They don't want their stomachs to come *near* anything called a solvent. The great minds of advertising have responded by coming up with new names for the solvent-using process. Since ethyl acetate is a naturally occurring substance in fruit, for example, publicists have begun to call coffee decaffeinated by this process *naturally* decaffeinated.

Traditional or European-process decaffeinated coffees continue to appear in stores because they're a bit cheaper than the water-only kind, and because some coffee professionals find that they better retain the characteristics of the original coffees.

The Sparkling-Water process (so-called because it uses water and CO_2, the two components of sparkling water), soaks the caffeine out of the beans with compressed carbon dioxide, a ubiquitous and altogether harmless substance. Essentially, the carbon dioxide first selectively removes the caffeine from the beans, then water removes the caffeine from the CO_2, in a continuous cycle. Eventually the virtually caffeine-free beans are removed from the cycle, dried, and sent out into the world for roasting.

Taste, Roast, and Decaffeination

However forcefully it may affect our nervous systems, caffeine has very little effect on flavor. Isolated, it is a bitter, almost tasteless white powder. Coffee without it should taste virtually the same as coffee with it.

Nevertheless, soaking green coffee beans in hot liquid and drying them again is not a gentle process. It definitely affects the flavor of the abused beans. Affects how much? Depending on how careful the decaffeination process and how attentive the subsequent roasting, from a little to a lot.

If you buy decaffeinated beans to roast at home you may notice that they are no longer the common gray-green color of unroasted coffee, but instead range from a rather sallow yellow to a light brown. This color change is owing to the soaking and drying to which the beans are subjected during decaffeination.

The result for roasting purposes is delicate beans that roast much less predictably than untreated beans. The combination of the loss of some flavor agents in the soaking process with the difficulty in roasting accounts for the fact that decaffeinated coffees purchased in the store may not taste as consistently good as coffee from untreated beans.

The main message for the home roaster is to buy green decaffeinated beans from a reliable source, and *roast them carefully*. See Chapter 5 and the instructions following that chapter for suggestions on handling decaffeinated coffees.

You might also consider making blends of decaffeinated and untreated coffees. The untreated beans bolster the taste of the decaffeinated beans, yet you still consume less caffeine. Remember, however, that you almost certainly will need to roast the decaffeinated beans in a separate session before blending, since they typically roast 15 to 25 percent faster than untreated beans.

I can't argue for or against any of the three principal decaffeination processes. I suspect that their success in not destroying the delicate aromatics that make coffee taste like coffee depends more on the care devoted to the process than to the process itself. Buy from a source that evaluates its coffees with taste and intelligence, and probably you will buy a good decaffeinated coffee regardless of process.

A nineteenth-century engraving of a Latin American coffee warehouse. It would appear to offer perfect conditions for storing green coffee: dark, as cool as the tropics permit, and presumably dry. In case you can't tell, the boss is the one counting the bags.

The Coffee Cellar

For food romantics *coffee cellar* has a fine ring. It resonates with the same combined pleasure of connoisseurship and security that motivates people to keep piles of dusty wine bottles deep in the hearts of their houses. The wine cellar, for all of its potential for snobbery and affectation, is a profoundly symbolic idea. It suggests that somewhere inside our being is a storehouse of pleasure that we can draw from to share and enjoy regardless of time, change, and the orneriness of the outside world.

The good news about coffee cellars is that home roasting makes it possible to have one. The bad news is that very little is documented or even generally known about the issues involved in the deliberate aging of coffee.

About storing coffee something is known. Correct storage for green coffees is cool but not cold, dark, dry, and well ventilated. Good, powerful green coffees kept in such conditions will change very little over the years. I recently cupped a Guatemalan Antigua I had held in dry, cool conditions for four years against a fresh new-crop Antigua; the four-year-old coffee to my palate was better than the new crop, although both were superb. The older coffee displayed just a touch of the taste I associate with proper aged coffees: a deepening body creating a sort of expansive resonance around the acidity.

But true aging in the Indonesian tradition remains a bit of a mystery. Coffees allowed to sit around in warehouses in port cities in Central America, for example, seem to go flat and dead rather rapidly, gaining some body but losing acidity and vitality. In the wonderful aged Sumatran coffees, however, the acidity emerges more alive than ever, wrapped inside the smooth, heavy body brought on by time.

So where are we with all of this? Here, I think. Stored in a cool, dry, dark, well-ventilated place "big" coffees—in other words, those that are not light, soft, or delicate to begin with—lose very little with storage and may subtly improve by gaining body. At what point do they finally go syrupy and dead, all body but no life? Common wisdom declares at ten to fifteen years, but I'm sure that the storage life of any particular coffee depends both on the coffee itself and on the conditions under which it is stored.

As for the secrets of true, deliberate aging as it's done in places like Sumatra, we probably will be forced to wait for science to catch up to tradition.

Since I live in San Francisco I can only store my coffee, not age it. If you live in the tropics, however, or close to them, you might conduct a few experiments of your own. Put some good green coffee in burlap, put it on a pallet in the carport, where the ventilation is good, and rotate the bags occasionally. Then write to me in time for my next book.

At any rate, cellaring coffees does not appear to offer quite the same clear and certain reward as cellaring wines. Nevertheless, you can enjoy coffees for some years after purchase, and come to know coffees in the rawness of youth, in the power of maturity, and in the deepness of age. Plus you can experiment with blends in ways that wine aficionados can't: Older coffees can balance younger, and vice versa.

Setting Up a Coffee Cellar

Again, green coffees should be stored (as opposed to deliberately aged) in a cool but not too cool, dry but not too dry, well-ventilated place that receives neither direct sunlight nor freezing temperatures. In fact, the sort of place that most of us would feel comfortable sleeping in: dark, about 65°F/15°C, with some air movement.

What kind of container should you store (or age) your coffee in? Your green coffee probably will appear packed in bags made of plastic or plastic-lined paper. Plastic is fine for short-term storage of smaller amounts of coffee, but if you plan to hold larger amounts for more than a month or two, you should transfer it to something porous. Cloth is doubtless best, but corrugated cardboard boxes probably will work as well.

Burlap bags of the kind used to construct temporary levees during periods of flood are ideal for storing or aging coffee at home. They are sold empty, they are a convenient size (not trivially small yet still luggable when full), and they include sewn-in drawstring closures. See Resources for suggestions on how to turn up a supply.

Green coffee is a living entity; it needs to breathe. Elevate the boxes or bags on a pallet or similar arrangement that allows air to circulate beneath them. Every few months shift the containers around. Turn them over, and if they are in a pile shift the bottom containers toward the top of the pile and bring the top ones down, much as you rotate tires on a car.

Fortunately for those of us who are weary of restaurants gotten up as strained imitations of wine cellars, there is no symbolic architecture associated with storing coffee beyond a simple warehouse filled with burlap coffee bags piled on pallets. So when it comes to the interior-design aspects of your coffee cellar (or coffee pantry), you are on your own.

Coffee Geography

Some Fancy Coffees of the World

Maps are the beloved vehicles of armchair traveling. Here are a few, accompanied by descriptions of coffees to taste in the armchair while looking over the maps.

Cartographic precision is hard to come by in the world of coffees. Most sources are vague, and few agree in detail. Consequently, I have fudged. If someone's farm is off in one of the white spaces, I apologize and invite correction.

Accompanying each map are brief descriptions of coffees that appear most frequently on the signs and lists of specialty coffee roasters and importers. I have omitted lesser-known coffees, some of which may be excellent but have not yet made an impression on North American markets.

The information in these descriptions is a condensed summary. For more information see the Philippe Jobin volume recommended in Resources. Also note that the increasing practice of marketing coffee by estate or cooperative means that we are likely to see more and more exceptions to the simple generalizations offered in this section.

Those simple generalizations are just that: cultural baggage that real experience drags along with it. All of the names, observations, and evaluations in this or any other book, not to mention various elegantly designed pamphlets on brown paper you may pick up in coffee stores, are meaningless unless they are confirmed by the senses— your senses. You need to experience these coffees, educate your taste, and ultimately trust it.

Finally, this summary and its evaluations do not take into account the human and political dimensions of coffee growing. They are based on the quality, taste characteristics, and availability of the coffees themselves. There may be reasons other than taste alone for choosing one coffee over another. For example, the embargo of Haiti in the early 1990s was particularly destructive to small Haitian coffee growers, who often were forced to burn their trees for charcoal in order to support their families, destroying both their livelihood and their land. Someone who cares about the overwhelming economic and ecological crisis the Haitian people are experiencing might well want to buy Haitian coffee in preference to similar coffees for humanitarian reasons. Analogous arguments might be made for buying Ethiopian coffees, cooperative coffees from Chiapas, or coffees of any number of other origins.

Mexico and Central America

Mexico. Most noted market names are Coatepec and Oaxaca; also Chiapas and Tapachula. Brisk, bright acidity, delicate flavor, medium body. Good blenders and dark roasters. Estates and several organic and progressive cooperatives. Some high-grown Mexican coffees may share the fuller body and richer acidity of the better Guatemalan coffees.

Guatemala. Distinctive rich acidity, often spicy or smoky, full body, big, complex flavor. The traditionally most favored regional marks are Antigua and Cobán, but many prefer Huehuetenango. Guatemala has tended to stand by the traditional old arabica varieties. With Mexico it remains one of the most reliable sources for the dramatically large beans of the Maragogipe, for example. Those interested in supporting small growers can look for coffees marketed by SCAG (Small Special Coffee Producers Association of Guatemala). Excellent estate coffees.

Honduras. Little coffee reaches the American specialty market. In general, smooth and unremarkable. Marcalas is probably the most distinguished market name.

El Salvador. Clean, mild acidity, delicate to bland flavor. An unobtrusive blender.

Nicaragua. Best (usually marked Matagalpa or Jinotega) tend to be good but unexceptional Central American coffees: medium body, decent acidity, straightforward taste.

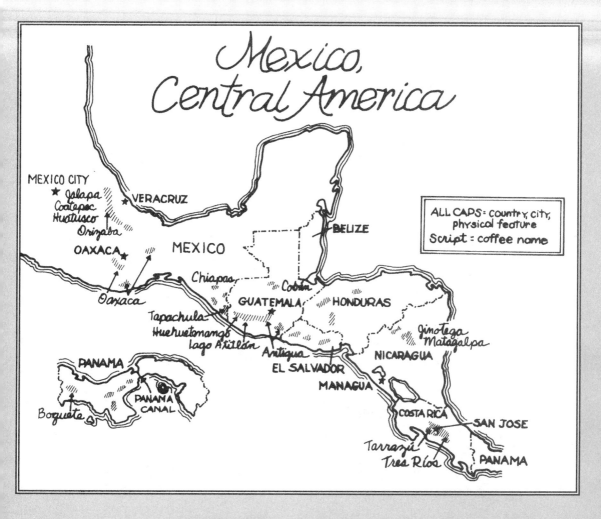

Mexico, Central America

ALL CAPS = country, city, physical feature
Script = coffee name

MEXICO CITY
★ Jalapa
Coatepec
Huatusco
Orizaba
VERACRUZ

OAXACA

MEXICO

BELIZE

Oaxaca

Chiapas

Cobán

GUATEMALA

HONDURAS

Tapachula

Jinotega
Matagalpa

Huehuetenango

Lago Atitlán

Antigua

NICARAGUA

EL SALVADOR

PANAMA

MANAGUA

Boquete

PANAMA
CANAL

COSTA RICA

SAN JOSE

Tarrazú
Tres Ríos

PANAMA

Costa Rica. Best (Tarrazú, Tres Ríos, other marks graded "strictly hard bean") are big, clean, with bright to rich acidity and full body. A variety of excellent estate coffees, including the celebrated La Minita. An association of small cooperatives exports its coffees under the mark Fedecoop. Warning: Although the finest Costa Rican coffees remain so, others may be clean tasting but lifeless, perhaps the result of plantings of new hybrids of arabica and careless processing practices.

Panama. Most are agreeable but not exceptional Central American coffees: medium body, brisk to delicate acidity. Others, particularly those from the Bouquete area near the Costa-Rican border, may display more power in the cup. Several excellent estates.

The Caribbean, Colombia, and Venezuela

Jamaica. True Jamaican Blue Mountain coffees (grown in the Blue Mountain district at over three thousand feet) are full-bodied, moderately acidy, complex yet balanced in taste. Lesser, lower-grown coffees (Blue Mountain Valley, High Mountain) are medium in body, delicate to bland in flavor, brisk rather than rich in acidity.

Haiti. When available, wet-processed Haitian coffee is typically sweet, soft, and medium-bodied. At this writing an association made up of several thousand small growers (Caféières Natives S.A.) is attempting to revive the Haiti coffee industry after its virtual destruction by the embargo of the early 1990s. The association's coffees are currently marketed under the name Haitian Bleu.

Dominican Republic (may be marketed as Santo Domingo). Higher-grown Dominican coffees, like Baní and Cibao Altura, can be fine examples of the Caribbean taste: soft, balanced, with a rich undercurrent of acidity. Lesser coffees may be mild and pleasant but lacking in acidity.

Puerto Rico. The revived Yauco Selecto is a splendid example of the Caribbean taste: full-bodied, balanced, and gentle, yet alive with a deep, vibrant complexity.

Colombia. Colombian coffee sold without qualifiers is usually MAM (acronym for three market names: Medellín-Armenia-Manizales), Excelso grade, most likely from trees of the Caturra or hybrid Colombiana varieties. Such generic Colombian coffee tends to range from clean and balanced in taste, reasonably rich in acidity, and full-bodied to flat and ordinary. The best Colombian (usually smaller lots from trees of the traditional Typica and Bourbon varieties, marketed by estate, association, or cooperative) is overwhelmingly rich in acidity, full-bodied, and powerfully aromatic.

Venezuela. Most coffee produced is consumed locally. When available, Venezuela from the coastal regions (often marked Caracas or sometimes Caripe) tends to reflect the Caribbean taste profile: mild, deep, low-toned, sweet. High-grown coffees from western Venezuela (Táchira, Mérida) resemble Colombian, and, in fact, may originate across the border in Colombia.

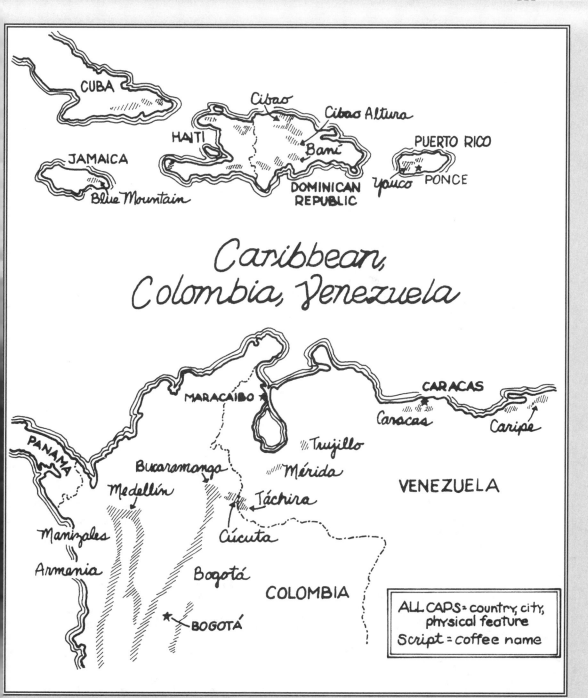

Caribbean, Colombia, Venezuela

CUBA

HAITI

JAMAICA

Blue Mountain

Cibao

Cibao Altura

Baní

DOMINICAN REPUBLIC

PUERTO RICO

Yauco   PONCE

PANAMA

MARACAIBO

Bucaramanga

Medellín

Manizales

Armenia

Cúcuta

Táchira

Trujillo

Mérida

Bogotá

BOGOTÁ

COLOMBIA

CARACAS

Caracas

Caripe

VENEZUELA

ALL CAPS = country, city, physical feature
Script = coffee name

South America

Ecuador.   Little Ecuadorian coffee reaches the North American specialty market. It typically is another smaller coffee in the classic Latin American style.

Peru.   Delicate to brisk acidity, medium body, sweet, mild flavor. Congenial blenders. Coffee is grown in the north (Northerns), center (Chanchamayo, Ayacucho), and south near Cuzco and Machu Picchu (Urubamba, Cuzco). Most admired name is probably Chanchamayo. Some organic and progressive cooperatives.

Brazil.   Brazil's enormous output of coffee varies just as enormously. Most Brazilian coffee is grown at relatively low elevations and dry-processed. If the picking and drying have been done carelessly

(ripe, overripe, and unripe beans all stripped from the trees and dried on the ground), the resulting bland- to medicinal-tasting coffee finds its way into the market category called "Brazils" and is used for instant coffees and cheap canned blends.

However, if the picking and drying are performed with care, these dry-processed beans will display the soft, earthy gentleness associated with the famous market name Santos. The better-quality, dry-processed Santos beans define the norm for good Brazilian coffee.

Other Brazilian coffees may be wet-processed or semiwashed. Typically, wet-processed Brazilian coffees display the brightest, cleanest taste with the most distinct acidity, the better dry-processed coffees exhibit fuller body and greater complexity but lower acidity, with semiwashed agreeably positioned between the two. Regardless of process, good Brazilian coffees tend to be mild, sweet, and medium-bodied, with a relatively delicate acidity, making them favorites for espresso blends and other dark roasting. A growing number of estates are attempting to establish identities on the North American market.

At one time the market name *Rios* referred to coffees shipped through Rio de Janeiro. Today the term (and its derivation *Rioy*) is used to describe Brazilian coffees, regardless of shipping point, that display a certain harsh, wild-to-medicinal taste. These "Rioy"-tasting coffees are almost never imported to the United States, although coffee drinkers in some parts of Europe enjoy their rough profile.

Yemen and East Africa

Yemen Mocha.   Rich, intense, winelike acidity; medium to full body; intriguing wild or natural notes. A remarkable coffee in the traditional, dry-processed style. Most Yemen coffee to reach North America is marked either Mattari or Sanani. Sanani is reputed to be more balanced, Mattari more acidy and distinctive.

Ethiopian dry-processed coffees.   Harar (also Harer, Harrar, Harrer) is medium-bodied, with fruity, winelike tones and some wild notes. An excellent, distinctive coffee often substituted for Yemen Mocha in good Mocha-Java blends. Gimbi (also Ghimbi), dry-processed or unwashed Jimma (also Djimah, Jima), and dry-processed Sidamo are usually lesser coffees, still wild and winy but lighter-bodied and rougher in profile than most Harar.

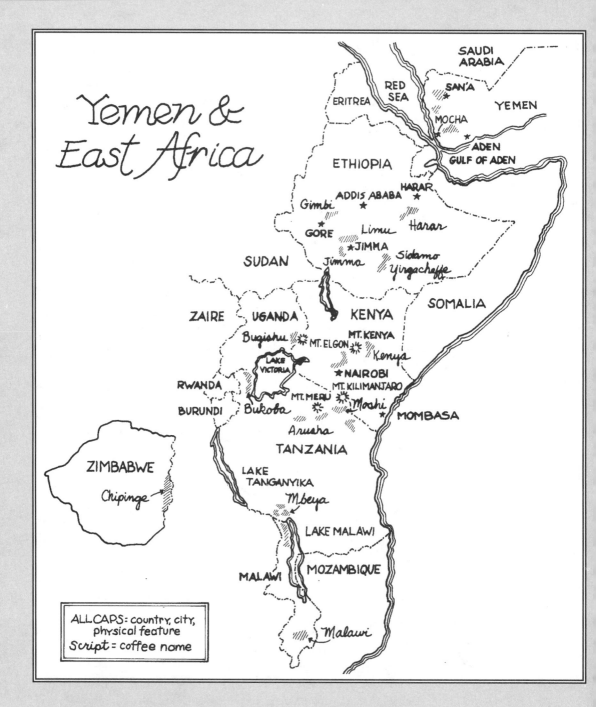

Yemen &
East Africa

SAUDI
ARABIA

ERITREA

RED
SEA

SAN'A ★

YEMEN

MOCHA

ADEN ★

GULF OF ADEN

ETHIOPIA

HARAR ★
ADDIS ABABA ★

Gimbi

GORE ★

Limu

Harar

JIMMA ★

Sidamo

Jimma

Yirgacheffe

SUDAN

ZAIRE

UGANDA

KENYA

SOMALIA

Bugishu

MT. ELGON ✳

MT. KENYA ✳

Kenya

LAKE
VICTORIA

★ NAIROBI

RWANDA

MT. KILIMANJARO ✳

BURUNDI

Bukoba

MT. MERU ✳

Moshi

MOMBASA ★

Arusha

TANZANIA

ZIMBABWE

Chipinge

LAKE
TANGANYIKA

Mbeya

LAKE MALAWI

MOZAMBIQUE

MALAWI

Malawi

ALL CAPS: country, city,
physical feature
Script = coffee name

Ethiopian wet-processed coffees. Yirgacheffe (also Yrgacheffe) is one of the world's most distinctive coffees: floral, fruity, with
rich, soft-toned acidity and substantial body. Coffee marked Limu and

the washed or wet-processed versions of Sidamo and Jimma are similar to Yirgacheffe but usually lighter-bodied and less intensely fruity.

Kenya. Kenya's centrally managed, aggressively up-to-date coffee industry still produces a splendid, consistent coffee, displaying a rich, powerful, winelike acidity wrapped inside a full body and complex taste. However, by all accounts, overall quality is beginning to slip as newer, hardier hybrids of arabica replace older varieties like Kent. Kenya coffee is sold at government auction by grade, regardless of region or botanical variety. The highest grade is AA, but specific lots of AA differ in quality and character. The government currently prohibits growers from identifying their coffee on the bag, but some exporters manage to buy identifiable lots and sell them by origin as premium versions of the Kenya taste.

Tanzania. The best Tanzanian coffees, grown mainly on the slopes of Mount Kilimanjaro and Mount Meru near the border with Kenya (usually marked Arusha, Moshi, or Kilimanjaro), resemble Kenyan coffees with their rich, winelike acidity and full body. Other wet-processed coffees, grown in the south near the town of Mbeya, tend to resemble the lesser Ethiopian wet-processed coffees: soft, ingratiatingly low-toned acidity, rounded taste, medium body. Dry-processed coffees grown near the western town of Bukoba are inexpensive "hard" arabicas that do not figure in the North American specialty trade.

Malawi. Those few Malawi coffees to reach North America recently resemble the softer, full-bodied washed coffees of Tanzania. Several estates.

Uganda. Ugandan Bugishu, grown on the slopes of Mount El-gon, resembles Kenya in general profile.

Zimbabwe. Zimbabwe is another version of the powerfully acidy, wine-toned, and full-bodied East African flavor profile. The Chipinge region on the eastern border with Mozambique produces the most and probably the best Zimbabwe coffee; 053 is the highest grade designation, based on size of bean. Several excellent estates. Farfell and Smaldeel have been most successful at establishing identities in the North American market.

India

India. Indian coffee is grown in the southern states of Karnataka, Tamil Nādu, and Kerala. Wet-processed Indian coffee (usually Plantation A grade, market name Mysore) is pleasant, low-keyed and sweet, with medium to full body. At best it resembles good Java and New Guinea coffees; at worst it may not display sufficient acidity to keep the coffee interesting. Coffees from the Shevaroys and Nilgiris districts may display brighter acidity; Cauvery Peaks Estate produces a coffee with interesting spicy tones.

Indian Monsooned Malabar. This is a dry-processed coffee exposed to monsoon winds in special warehouses on the southeastern coast of India before export. It displays a unique taste profile: heavy on the palate, with a peculiar muted acidity. Its low-key heaviness makes it attractive to some espresso blenders.

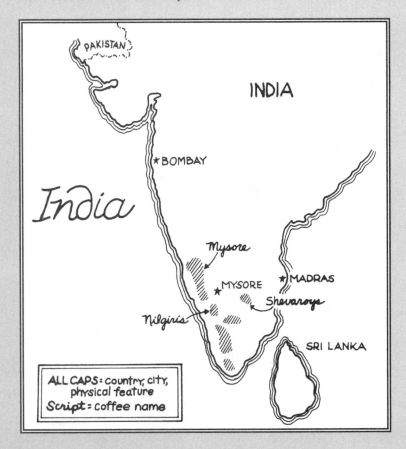

Indonesia, New Guinea, and Hawaii

Sumatra. The best (marked Mandheling or Lintong, from the region just inland from the southern coast about one hundred miles directly south of the city of Medan) are among the world's most distinctive coffees, with a rich, resonant, deep-toned acidity, full body, and occasional winelike notes. It appears that the true, traditional Lintong and Mandheling coffees are semiwashed, but reliable information on these origins is difficult to come by. As Sumatran coffees become better documented, the full range of local processing and handling methods may be intelligently reflected in coffee literature.

Coffees grown farther west, at the tip of the island in the Aceh region, are usually marked Gayo Mountain. These coffees appear to be processed and handled differently from the traditional Lintong and Mandheling origins and may derive from newer varieties of Arabica. At this writing they are cleaner, lighter, and less resonant in the cup than the full-flavored beans for which Sumatra is famous.

Sulawesi (Celebes). The best Sulawesi coffees display the same deep, rich flavor profile as traditional Sumatran coffees, although they may be slightly lighter in body and more high-toned in their acidity. The Toraja region, in the southeast finger of the island, about one hundred miles north of the port city Ujung Pandang or Makasar, is the source of most fine Sulawesi coffee. Coffee from Toraja also may be marketed as Kalossi or Kalosi, the old, colonial Dutch name for the Toraja region. Thus the descriptions "Celebes Kalossi" and "Sulawesi Toraja" are essentially interchangeable. Several estates.

Java. All higher-quality arabica coffee from Java is wet-processed. Possibly because wet processing simplifies its taste, Java coffees tend to be lesser versions of the best Sumatran and Sulawesi coffees. Body may not be as heavy, and the rich, low-toned acidity still satisfying but not so vibrant. There are five traditional government-sponsored estates, the best-known of which are Jampit and Blawan, plus additional private estates.

Bali. Relatively little Bali coffee reaches North American markets owing to its popularity among Japanese buyers.

Papua New Guinea. The best coffees of Papua New Guinea are superb variations on the Malay Archipelago flavor profile: a bit

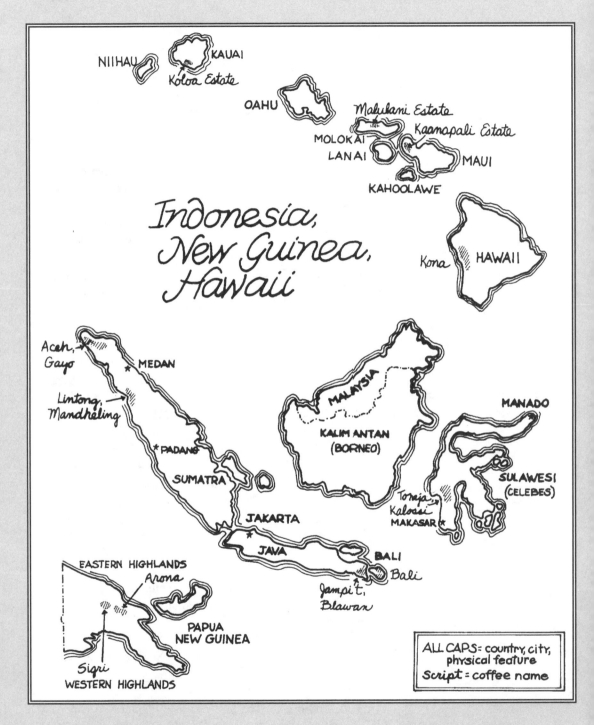

NIIHAU   KAUAI
        Koloa Estate

OAHU   Malukani Estate
                Kaanapali Estate
        MOLOKAI
        LANAI   MAUI
            KAHOOLAWE

Indonesia,
New Guinea,
Hawaii   Kona   HAWAII

Aceh,
Gayo   MEDAN

Lintong,   MALAYSIA   MANADO
Mandheling
                        KALIMANTAN
                        (BORNEO)
        PADANG
                                            SULAWESI
SUMATRA   (CELEBES)

                                Toraja
                                Kalossi
                JAKARTA   MAKASAR

                        JAVA   BALI
                                    Bali
EASTERN HIGHLANDS   Jampit,
        Arona   Blawan

                PAPUA
                NEW GUINEA
                                ALL CAPS = country, city,
Sigri   physical feature
WESTERN HIGHLANDS   Script = coffee name

lighter-bodied and higher-toned than the best Sumatra and Sulawesi, with a wonderfully floral acidity and a delicate sweetness. All are wet-processed, typically with great care. Currently the most prominent estates are Arona and Sigri. The highest grade is AA.

Australia. Most of Australia's coffee production is consumed at home. An estate coffee recently available in North American markets displays good body but lacks the acidity and complexity of the better Indonesian archipelago coffees.

Hawaii. The celebrated Kona coffees are grown on the west coast of the big island of Hawaii. They resemble classic Latin American coffees like Costa Rican more than they do Indonesian or New Guinea coffees. They are always clean and balanced, but at best display a superb, rich, high-toned acidity, medium to full body, and complex aroma. The Kona coast is turning into the Napa Valley of coffee growing, as an increasing number of excellent small estates compete for the attention of both coffee roasters and tourists. Growers are now producing coffees on other islands in the Hawaiian chain. Maui, Kauai, and Molokai all support interesting and improving estate coffees.

Getting Started

Equipment, Methods, Issues

Despite the simplicity of the requirements, at this writing the home-appliance world still has not given us an effective, inexpensive home roasting device. Consequently, most approaches described here are improvisations. They will produce excellent coffee, however.

I have not presented every possible approach. Until recently home roasting persisted in North America as the private, isolated passion of the dedicated few, and every one of those dedicated few seemed convinced that his or her method was the only method that had ever been invented. I seldom made a public appearance at a book or coffee store without someone's sidling up and confiding his or her roasting routine to me, delighted to find a kindred spirit, but also shocked to discover that there were other ways to do it.

I have tried every home-roasting method I've heard of plus some I've only heard about in my dreams. A few simply don't work; I can only conclude that the people who use them are baking their coffee rather than roasting it. However, I have left out a few methods that do work.

I've left out the simplest approach of all, which is simply dumping the beans in a skillet and stirring them until they're brown. This method does roast coffee, just as it did for hundreds of years before people started inventing machines to do it better. But the coffee produced by skillet roasting surely will disappoint twentieth-century sophisticates, who have come to expect something tastier than the scorched and uneven beans that satisfied our eighteenth-century forebears.

When I published my first book on coffee twenty years ago I proposed a variation on the simple skillet approach: standing an oven thermometer inside a lightweight frying pan with a tight-fitting lid. The oven thermometer tells you about when the interior of the pan is hot enough to properly roast the beans, and the pan is light enough to enable you to shake the beans rather than stir them, which helps prevent scorching.

Some years ago I was delighted to discover that someone had adapted this method for a home-roasting kit. The Agape Coffee Beans Kit added some useful nuances to the idea, and presented it attractively. Since then I've run into people who have added still more wrinkles to the technique.

It's a workable way to roast coffee at home, but I haven't included it here for the simple reason that the modified stove-top corn popper described later in this chapter works even better.

Finally, there are some approaches to home-roasting that require considerable work with tools to transform apparatus intended for other purposes into devices that will roast coffee. It is possible to add a roasting chamber to the end of a heat gun, for example, an idea originated by Michael Sivetz, the fluid-bed roasting pioneer. I have discovered that rotisserie attachments to outdoor gas grills can be fitted with a tumble basket lined with aluminum screening, thus creating an ad hoc roasting drum that rotates under the grill cover on the rotisserie shaft. But both of these approaches involve so much careful work with tools that they seem to qualify more as home handi-craftsperson projects than home-roasting techniques, so I have omitted them.

So after that preamble, here are the goods. To save you the need to make notes or turn over the corners of pages, the important practical information contained in this chapter is summarized in list/recipe format in the section titled "Quick Guide to Home-Roasting Procedure" on pages 150–172.

Roasting Requirements

By way of orientation, let's review what needs to take place in coffee roasting:

- The beans must be subjected to temperatures between 370°F/190°C and 540°F/280°C. Faster air currents permit lower roasting temperatures, and vice versa. Thus fluid-bed devices, including hot-air corn poppers, roast at lower temperatures than do gas ovens or stove-top corn poppers.

- The beans (or the air around them) must be kept moving to avoid uneven roasting or scorching.

- The roasting must be stopped at the right moment and the beans cooled promptly.

- Some provision must be made to vent the roasting smoke.

Here are some ways to achieve these simple goals at home. All have their advantages and disadvantages.

Stove-Top Roasting

Until a few years ago traditional cast-iron stove-top coffee roasters (they looked like heavy covered saucepans with cranks on top) still could be purchased through Italian importers. Now these picturesque devices appear to be permanently and finally out of production.

The most readily available substitute is the stove-top corn popper, the kind that looks like a covered saucepan with a crank protruding from the top. The crank turns a pair of wire vanes that rotate just above the bottom of the pan, agitating the corn kernels (in our case the coffee beans) to keep them from scorching.

There are several stove-top poppers on the market at this writing, but the one that I find works best for coffee roasting is the Felknor International Theater II. The suggestions and instructions for stove-top roasting here (and on pages 150–153) are all based on my experience with the Theater II popper.

Do not buy the somewhat similar West Bend electric countertop Stir Crazy corn popper to roast coffee, by the way. It does not generate quite enough heat; it bakes coffee rather than roasting it.

Although the manufacturer obviously designed the Theater II to pop corn rather than roast coffee, it actually turns out to be superior to traditional stove-top coffee roasters in two respects. First, it permits easy access to the beans. With the Theater II, half of the lid opens and folds back, making dumping the beans and keeping an eye on them while they're roasting relatively simple. A second advantage to the Theater II is the ease with which it can be modified to accept an inexpensive candy thermometer. The candy thermometer provides rough readings of the temperature inside the popper, allowing you to safely and decisively manipulate burner settings to maintain optimum temperatures during the roast. Adding a candy thermometer to the Theater II is a very easy procedure, requiring only a drill, a single drill

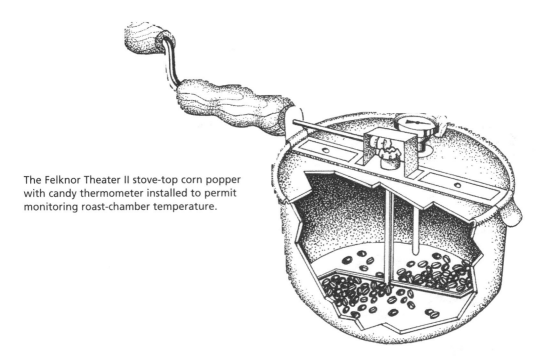

The Felknor Theater II stove-top corn popper with candy thermometer installed to permit monitoring roast-chamber temperature.

bit, some odd nuts and washers as spacers, and about two minutes of elementary fiddling.

The body of the Theater II popper is constructed of aluminum, however, and like all light-bodied aluminum cookware it eventually will melt if held empty over high heat for an extended period of time. Not that the Theater II is shabbily made. It is very well made, and if used following the instructions in this book will last through years of coffee roasting. But for those who read quickly or are inattentive I offer the following warning: *Never use a stove-top corn popper on burner settings above medium (with an electric range) or low (with a gas range), and never leave the popper unattended with the heat on.*

Given that, I find the Theater II popper does an excellent job. I've tasted coffees roasted in it against equally fresh, professionally roasted coffees from the same crop and found the Theater II–roasted beans often better than their professionally roasted counterparts, and at worst only slightly inferior in acidity and aroma. The edge in home-roasted freshness will completely outweigh any such slight deficiencies. And the Theater II roasts a half-pound of coffee per session, so you needn't hover over the stove cranking all that often.

Detailed instructions for using the Theater II appear on pages 150–153. If you have trouble finding the Theater II see Resources for ordering information.

Fluid-Bed Approaches

Fluid-bed roasting means the beans are both roasted and agitated by a powerful current of hot air, much as hot-air corn poppers heat and agitate corn kernels.

Two approaches are possible. First, you can buy *the recommended design* of hot-air corn popper and use it to roast coffee. It will work well and will cost under $25. If you fit your popper with a candy-thermometer heat probe as described in the section following this

The Arabian coffee ceremony. The word *ceremony* may have originated with European commentators, who remarked on the similarities between this Arab (and the similar Ethiopian and Eritrean) practices to the better-known Japanese tea ceremony. The coffee ceremony is a bit less formal than its tea-drinking counterpart, but also technically more complex, since the coffee is not only brewed and drunk during the course of the event, but roasted and ground as well. Here the coffee beans, having already been roasted, are being pulverized in an ornate wooden mortar, while water for brewing is being heated in the open fire pit. The long-handled roasting ladle and spatula for stirring the roasting beans are neatly laid out on the far edge of the fire pit. From an early twentieth-century photograph.

chapter, you will have a home roaster that in certain respects is more sophisticated than the typical sample roaster used by professionals.

Second, you can buy a fluid-bed device specifically designed to roast coffee at home. Unfortunately, at this writing the selection of such devices is limited. The only regularly available options are a heavily modified corn popper and a converted heat gun, both relatively expensive and only marginally superior to an ordinary, unmodified hot-air popper. This situation may change soon, however, as at least three manufacturers have developed prototypes and are eyeing the market. These new devices will work almost exactly like hot-air poppers but will incorporate amenities like built-in cooling cycles, timing devices to automatically terminate the roast, and in the case of one of the prototypes, a glass roasting chamber permitting easy observation of the roasting beans.

Roasting with Hot-Air Corn Poppers

Both hot-air corn poppers and home fluid-bed roasters produce a very consistent, uniform roast, with bright acidity, good aroma, and a clean taste. The body may be slightly lighter than in coffees roasted by other methods, and the taste perhaps less complex. Dark roasts gotten by fluid-bed methods will be somewhat pungent and sharp compared to dark roasts achieved by other home methods.

Fluid-bed roasters present particular issues in regard to chaff, the tiny, paperlike flakes of coffee-fruit skin liberated by roasting. On the positive side, these devices blow the chaff up and out of the coffee beans while roasting them. On the negative side, the chaff blown out of the beans by the fluid-bed method tends to float around the kitchen and complicate housekeeping. The plastic hoods that fit over the tops of hot-air poppers provide a fairly effective method for corralling the chaff, however, and any home fluid-bed roaster designed from scratch that appears after this writing undoubtedly will incorporate a baffle or filter that collects the chaff.

An inexpensive, attractive chaff-filtering device that fits over the top of hot-air poppers may be heading toward the market as this book goes to press. The manufacturer plans to call it the MacCochran roasting adaptor. It looks something like a large candlesnuffer. An electrostatic filter traps the chaff and a clear plastic window permits you to monitor the developing color of the beans inside the roasting/popping chamber. See page 42 for the patent illustration. This device is useful, handsome, and will make an excellent gift for the coffee fanatic in your circle. Nevertheless, don't feel that you need to wait for it to appear before beginning to roast in a hot-air popper.

A more important issue with hot-air poppers is the remote danger of combustion chaff may pose with some designs. *Use only poppers of the design illustrated on page 154 for home coffee roasting;* in other words, use those machines that introduce the hot air from the sides of the popping/roasting chamber. *Do not use designs in which the hot air issues from screened or grill-covered openings or slots directly on the bottom of the popping/roasting chamber.* Not only are such styles ineffective coffee roasters, but they also pose the possibility that fragments of the roasting chaff could settle into the base of the popper, collect around the heating elements, and eventually cause the device to ignite. I have heard of only one such incident, but even one is enough to invite caution.

Also keep in mind that if you use any unmodified hot-air popper for coffee roasting you void its warranty by employing it for a purpose other than the one for which it was originally intended. The recommended designs are sturdy as well as inexpensive, however, and stand up well to roasting. Only if you regularly produce very dark (dark French or Italian) roasts are you likely to dramatically shorten the life of your popper. If you enjoy these extremely dark roasts you should probably learn to use a stove-top roaster.

There are two other advantages to hot-air poppers. The first is the ease with which they can be modified to incorporate a metal candy/deep-fry thermometer. This simple (two-minute) modification enables you to monitor the progress of the roast by the inner temperature of the beans rather than by their outer appearance. Note that this utilization of a candy/deep-fry thermometer differs from its use in the stove-top corn-popper method described earlier. With the stove-top popper the thermometer is used to measure the temperature of the roast chamber rather than the temperature of the beans themselves, as is proposed here.

The second advantage of the hot-air popper is its usefulness in preparing small, consistent samples of coffee for systematic tasting and evaluation. See the afterword on home coffee cupping.

A final note on hot-air poppers: These devices incorporate two safety devices to prevent overheating. One is a fuselike component that shuts the machine down permanently if it malfunctions. The other is a thermostat that temporarily cuts off current if the machine moderately overheats, then relents after the machine has cooled again. If you are roasting several batches of coffee in succession, you

The Sirocco home roaster, a small fluid-bed roaster manufactured in Germany and imported to the United States throughout the late 1970s and 1980s. Its cooling cycle is conveniently activated by a timer. A paper filter in the metal chaff collector atop the glass roasting chamber helps control roasting smoke. The Sirocco is no longer manufactured. At this writing only a few units are available; they are expensive and in odd voltages.

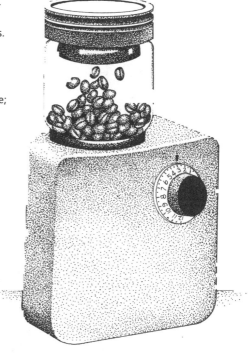

may shut down the machine by triggering the second, temporary switch. Simply allow the unit to cool, then resume roasting.

Complete instructions for using the appropriate designs of hot-air corn popper to roast coffee appear on pages 154–158, together with directions for adding a candy thermometer should you wish to.

Home Fluid-Bed Roasters

As I write we are in an awkward hiatus in the history of built-from-scratch home fluid-bed roasters. The old ones have largely vanished from the market and the new ones haven't yet appeared.

Until recently a well-designed home fluid-bed roaster was available on the American market, though at a relatively high price. It incorporated a cooling cycle controlled by mechanical timer and paper filters to contain chaff and help control roasting smoke. This German-manufactured device, distributed under a variety of names but best known as the Sirocco roaster, is now out of production, probably permanently. A few odd units wired for foreign voltages are still available at this writing (see Resources). A little underpowered roaster imported by Melitta during the 1980s was run off the shelves by American patent-holders, probably fortunately so given its limitations.

New fluid-bed machines configured much like the Sirocco, with visually accessible roasting chambers, chaff collectors, and cooling cycles activated by mechanical timers, should be on the market sometime in 1997. Based on the various prototypes I've seen, these units will be technically superior to the Sirocco, but will sell for considerably less. See page 41 for a patent drawing and description of one proposed machine. Additional fluid-bed devices from other manufacturers also could be on the way.

However, at the moment the only regularly available alternative to an ordinary hot-air popper for those who wish to explore fluid-bed roasting is a hot-air popper that has been professionally modified for coffee roasting, the Sivetz home roaster, manufactured and distributed via the mails by fluid-bed roasting pioneer Michael Sivetz. The Sivetz device has a lovable Rube Goldberg look, roasts one-third pound of beans per session, incorporates a cooling cycle, and includes a metal candy thermometer pressed into service as a heat probe to measure the internal heat of the mass of roasting beans. The temperature-monitoring capability of the Sivetz machine will endear it to those technically inclined readers who prefer system over the senses. However, the lack of any means of controlling floating chaff will not endear it to those who clean house, which means the Sivetz roaster is best used in a basement or on a back porch. Like ordinary, unmodified hot-air poppers, the Sivetz device strains to produce a very dark (dark French or Italian) roast, but turns out lovely versions of the moderately dark to dark roasts used for espresso. The advantages of the rather expensive Sivetz machine over unmodified poppers are its cooling cycle and somewhat greater bean capacity. Its disadvantage, once again, is its prodigality with chaff. With ordinary poppers the plastic hood or chute that fits over the top of the popping chamber can be used to divert the floating chaff down into a bowl. With the Sivetz modification, the hood is gone and the chaff floats majestically free.

Sivetz also manufactures two fluid-bed roasters based on heat guns. A heat gun is a tool that looks and works like a high-powered hair drier and is used for tasks like softening and removing paint. It produces a very powerful jet of air at temperatures that are both high and adjustable, all of which would seem to make it an ideal base for small-scale, fluid-bed coffee roasting. Unfortunately, the Sivetz modifications roast only 1 ounce and 2½ ounces of coffee per session respectively, and both models need to be hand-held during operation.

Their adjustable heat makes them an interesting experimental tool for the more experienced home roaster, but their small capacity, coupled with the handling they require during operation, would seem to render them impractical appliances for everyday use.

General advice for using small fluid-bed roasters can be found in the instructions following this chapter. For ordering information on the Sivetz machines and the remaining Sirocco home roasters, plus contact numbers for new units, see Resources.

Home-Roasting Apparatus of the Future (or Present)

From my knowledge of current patents and manufacturers' plans I can predict with confidence that home-roasting devices of the immediate future will employ fluid-bed technology; in other words they will work much like hot-air corn poppers with added features specifically designed for coffee roasting.

As you read this book that future may have already arrived; sleek new fluid-bed roasters may be on the shelves singing their songs of desire to passing consumers. To be worth their purchase price these devices should incorporate the following features:

- A cooling cycle that can be activated manually and/or automatically by timer.

- A filter or other device to control and collect roasting chaff.

- Easy visual access to roasting beans or other effective means of monitoring the progress of the roast (a thermometer acting as heat probe, for example).

- A capacity of at least three (preferably four or more) ounces of green beans by weight per session.

Lastly, if you are a lover of darker roasts or espresso cuisine you should make certain that the fluid-bed roaster you purchase will produce darker roasts without straining.

Any roasting device that does not incorporate all of these features may not be a significant improvement on the improvised methods described in this chapter.

If such a wonderful, coffee-fanatic-fulfilling appliance does appear, it definitely will be more than worth its purchase price. However, its sheer existence does not necessarily make other methods, like stove-top or gas-oven, obsolete. Not only do the stove-top and oven approaches roast more coffee per session, but they also produce different styles of roast, styles that some aficionados may prefer to the straightforward, brighter taste of fluid-bed coffee.

Again, general advice for using home fluid-bed roasters appears in the instructions following this chapter.

At least one home roaster being manufactured in Europe uses infrared radiation. The beans rest on a perforated, vibrating tray under an infrared heating element. Presumably the vibration agitates the beans sufficiently to maintain an even roast. You manage the cooling yourself by dumping the beans into a colander or bowl, just as you would with other home roasting methods. The Damm Costa Rica Home Roaster prepares only $1\frac{1}{2}$ ounces of beans per session, but offers adjustable heat settings. The manufacturer claims that the infrared elements burn off most roasting smoke. I am introducing the Costa Rica here, as a home roaster of the future, because no American importer has picked it up yet, doubtless because current models operate on 240 volts, and more to the point, because this attractive appliance carries a current suggested retail price of $1000. Well-heeled home-roasting pioneers interested in trying the Costa Rica machine will find the Damm Kaffeeröstsysteme address in the contact information in Resources.

As home roasting grows in popularity retreads of traditional designs like the little counter-top electric drum roasters pictured on page 40 also may appear. I can even imagine a market for the picturesque ball roasters that sit atop stove burners, a modern equivalent of the devices pictured near the bottom of page 39. If such old-time apparatus does show up on the shelves or in catalogs, look for the following design features:

- Easy visual access to roasting beans.

- Easy means of dumping roasted beans.

If the heat source is built into the device, make certain it reaches temperatures sufficient to bring coffee to a medium roast within a minimum of fifteen minutes. Ideally, the heat source should be adjustable.

Of course such traditional devices may be so charming in appearance and nostalgic in operation that you may decide to put up with a few awkward features. After all, people still wade on slippery rocks and flail away with fly rods when they could just go to the market and buy a trout. Sometimes the difficulties are half the fun.

For advice on using traditional stove-top or counter-top drum and ball apparatus, consult the relevant procedure for stove-top roasting in the instructions that follow this chapter, pages 150–153.

Roasting in Gas and Convection Ovens

Two kinds of ovens can be used to roast coffee: most ordinary kitchen gas ovens and some electric convection ovens. Microwave ovens cannot be used for coffee roasting. Conventional electric ovens, including toaster ovens, can be used but produce extremely uneven roasts. I do not recommend them, but if you wish to try roasting in one, simply follow the instructions for gas ovens.

Roasting in a Gas Oven

A single layer of coffee beans spread densely over a perforated surface will permit the gentle air currents moving inside gas ovens to flow through the beans and roast them fairly evenly. Palani Plantation produces an excellent, inexpensive device especially designed for this style of roasting, but most general-purpose perforated baking pans work equally well. Some beans will roast more darkly than others, but (this will sound like heresy to many professionals) I'm not sure that matters. In fact, the added complexity achieved by mixing beans brought to slightly varying degrees of roast in the same cup often dramatically enhances flavor. During my experiments with gas ovens I've turned out some rather funky-looking roasts that have tasted superb, with a wide, deep flavor palate that few professional roasts I've tasted have ever matched.

It is true, however, that achieving an acceptable roast in a given gas oven usually requires patient experiment with that particular appliance. And precise control of roast style can be difficult under any circumstances. This means that gas oven roasting may not be a good idea for those who prefer roast styles at the very light or the very dark ends of the spectrum, since with a light roast some beans may hardly be roasted at all, while at the dark end some beans may end up virtually burned. But for those who prefer medium through moderately dark styles, gas-oven roasting can produce a remarkably rich, complex cup, a gustatory surprise that can only be experienced through home roasting.

Monitoring the progress of the roast also can be tricky with an oven, since the smoke and crackling that signal the onset of pyrolysis are muted by the barrier of the oven door, and you may need to use a flashlight to check the color of the beans as you peek inside.

Nevertheless, the flexible, precise control of temperature provided by gas ovens is an advantage, as are the venting arrangements, which carry the roasting smoke outside, usually with considerable efficiency. Gas ovens will roast a pound or more of coffee at a time, more than most other methods.

Detailed instructions for gas-oven roasting appear on pages 161–166.

Roasting in an Electric Convection Oven

Ordinary electric ovens do not generate sufficient air movement to roast coffee evenly, but many convection ovens, which bake by means of rapidly moving currents of heated air, can be pressed into service as ad hoc coffee roasters.

The majority of convection ovens manufactured today have a maximum heat setting of 450°F/230°C. This temperature is barely enough to bring coffee beans to a proper roast. Smaller convection ovens, those that resemble toaster ovens, typically have maximum settings lower than 450°F/230°C, and cannot be used successfully. Those few ovens built with a maximum setting of 500°F/260°C or higher usually will produce a good, if mild-tasting, roast.

If you own a convection oven, test its heat output with an oven thermometer before attempting to use it to roast coffee. Instructions for this simple evaluation are given on pages 166–169, along with detailed instructions for convection-oven roasting. If you decide to purchase a convection oven especially for use in roasting coffee, look for a model that provides a maximum heat setting of 500°F/260°C or higher and permits easy visual inspection of the roasting beans through nontinted glass.

Even those convection ovens that generate reasonable roast temperatures tend to produce long, slow roasts of eighteen to twenty-five minutes. This deliberate pace yields a rather mild-tasting coffee with low acidity and muted aroma in the middle range of the roast spectrum and a rather sweet, gentle profile in dark roasts. Some coffee drinkers, particularly those who take their coffee black and unsweetened, may prefer the taste of coffee roasted in a convection oven to the more complex, acidy taste of coffees roasted by other methods. And those few Americans who sip their espresso straight, without frothed milk, also may find the smooth flavor profile of convection-oven dark roasts attractive. However, I suspect that the majority of American coffee fanciers will find convection-oven coffee bland.

Ovens with Combined Thermal and Convection Functions

Some sophisticated electric ovens now convert from conventional operation to convection mode at the touch of a button. Such ovens also permit simultaneous use of both conventional and convection functions. For coffee roasting the combination setting works best. Complete instructions for roasting with these versatile devices is included with the instructions for general oven roasting on pages 161–166.

Higher-Priced Professional Equipment

For the serious aficionado, professional sample roasters and small shop machines may offer an interesting alternative despite their high price.

Classic cylinder sample roasters, updated versions of the machines used for over a hundred years by professionals to prepare green coffee for cupping, can be had for around $3,500. Most require either a gas hookup, propane, or a 220-volt outlet. For an idea of how these handsome, romantic, and very durable devices look and operate, turn to the illustration on page 64.

Small tabletop fluid-bed and convection shop machines typically run on electric current alone, but sell for $7,000 and up, probably putting them out of range of any but the most dedicated hobbyist-aficionado.

See Resources for information on obtaining small-scale professional roasting equipment.

Style of Roast

Different roasts for different folks. Some prefer a light-colored, acidy, almost sour roast. Others prefer a dark-colored, oily, nearly burned style. Between, the classicists range themselves, from brisk medium roasts to a rich but balanced espresso. To review how these roast styles work out in terms of taste and terminology see the chart on pages 68–69.

The simplest way to translate your personal taste in roast into home practice is to find a store that sells a whole-bean coffee roasted in a style you like, buy some, and attempt to duplicate it at home.

However, those who want to fully explore the nuances of home roasting may prefer to carry out systematic experiments to determine their tastes in roast, and along the way learn in detail about green coffees and roast styles. See pages 140–149 near the end of this chapter for suggestions on how to carry out such experiments.

Timing the Roast

As with poaching eggs or cooking pasta, the main trick with roasting coffee is knowing when to stop.

Coffee roasting is considerably more forgiving in this respect than many kitchen procedures. With fresh pasta, for example, a thirty-second distraction can turn *al dente* into *al mush*, whereas with coffee roasting a minute or two delay merely produces a darker roast that is still drinkable and enjoyable.

The following section offers an orientation to the issues involved in timing a roast. Detailed and sequential instructions for various specific home-roasting procedures are given in the section following this chapter.

By Instrument or by Senses

For home as well as professional roasters there are two basic ways to time a roast: by instrument and by observation.

In this case "instrument" means a heat probe or thermometer incorporated into the roasting apparatus. The thermometer measures the approximate internal temperature of the roasting beans. Since internal bean temperature is a measurement of roast style (see the chart on pages 68–69), the reading on the heat probe will inform the operator when to conclude a roast so as to achieve a given style.

Unfortunately, the instrument approach is difficult to realize with most home-roasting methods. Inexpensive metal thermometers intended for candy making and deep frying can be used to measure bean temperature in hot-air poppers by means of a very simple, two-minute modification. A candy thermometer also is standard equipment with the Sivetz home roaster described on pages 158–161. With those two exceptions using candy thermometers to measure bean temperature (as distinct from roast-chamber temperature as in the proposed modifications to the Theater II stove-top roaster) involves extensive and rather clumsy alterations to equipment that go beyond the scope of this book.

Look, Smell, and Listen

So you need to learn to read the roast with your senses, as most roasters have done throughout history. The principles are simple: look, smell, and listen.

For the looking part you will need some sample beans, already roasted to the color you prefer, to which you compare the color of your own beans as they roast and gradually deepen in color. You place these sample beans where you can see them easily during the roasting session.

After you begin the roasting process, nothing dramatic will happen for some three to ten minutes (or even longer in the case of convection ovens) while a grassy or burlaplike odor rises from the beans. You needn't watch the beans during this early stage of the roast, but if you do you will notice that they are changing in color from a gray green to a light golden brown. The exceptions are decaffeinated and aged coffees, which start out a lightish brown and gradually darken.

In some cases your observations also may be confused by the thin, light-colored skin that covers some beans, called silverskin before roasting and chaff after. When you are monitoring roast color, ignore these large flakes, which will remain a light brown color regardless of how dark the rest of the bean becomes.

Eventually steam, still smelling like grass or burlap, will begin rising from the beans. Gradually this steam will darken and take on a coffeelike odor. On the heels of the appearance of the darker, coffee-smelling roasting smoke you will hear a subdued crackling sound, confirming the onset of pyrolysis, or the inner transformation of the bean.

From this moment forward you must depend mainly on sight. Assuming your goal is a medium to medium-dark roast, wait about thirty seconds to a minute after the crackling sets in and begin peeking at the beans to monitor their color. How soon after the onset of pyrolysis you need to start your visual inspection of the beans depends partly on how dark you want to roast, and partly on the roasting method you're using. Roasts develop rather quickly in hot-air corn poppers and very slowly in convection ovens, with stove-top and gas-

oven roasting ranged somewhere between. Again, specific suggestions on timing are given for each method in the roasting instructions
following this chapter.

With dark roasts your ear and nose may offer additional assistance.
As coffee passes from a medium roast to the slightly darker roast usually called full city, the roasting smoke increases in volume and subtly
changes in odor, while the crackling sound, which tends to diminish or
stop altogether during the middle ranges of roast color, starts to inten-
sify again. This "second crack," together with the fuller, more pungent
roasting smoke, can be a reliable indicator to an experienced home
roaster that the time is approaching to conclude a dark roast.

Regardless of whether you are pursuing a lighter or darker roast
you will need to observe the beans visually as they approach the crit-
ical moment when they match the color of your sample. When they
are about the same or a little lighter than your sample you must stop
the roast and begin the cooling process, usually by dumping the roasting beans into a colander or bowl. I realize that "the same or a little
lighter" is hardly precise language, but you'll learn.

Whichever roasting method you use or roast style you prefer, you
will eventually develop a feel for timing through experience with your
particular method and equipment. Again, only our general unfamiliar-
ity with roasting technique makes these instructions any more intimi-
dating than directions for broiling a steak or preparing eggs over easy.

An obvious warning: *Never leave roasting beans unattended.* This
is a particularly important caution with the stove-top and hot-air-
popper methods. With these approaches you should not even leave
the room until the heat is off and the session over. If coffee beans are
abandoned inside a hot roasting chamber long enough, they become
semiflammable—not nearly as dangerous as many foods become
when left over heat, but flammable nevertheless.

The gas-oven and convection methods allow you a bit more lee-
way. By controlling the variables discussed later in this chapter and
keeping a few simple records, it is possible to determine *approximately*
when to end a roasting session by elapsed time, thus permitting the use
of a kitchen timer to alert you to the impending moment of truth.

Concluding and Cooling the Roast

Cooling the hot beans rapidly and efficiently is one of the most
important steps in home roasting, since coffee continues to roast from
its own internal heat long after it has been removed from external

Kicking off the cooling process for just-roasted beans with a few one-second bursts of purified water, applied with a very fine spray. Done correctly, such *water quenching* will improve the quality of the roast by decisively initiating cooling. Done incorrectly, it can harm the roast by promoting staling. See pages 169–171 for complete instructions.

heat. Coffee that is allowed to coast down to room temperature of its own accord will taste dramatically inferior to coffee that is promptly and decisively cooled.

Many home roasters prepare small batches of a few ounces of beans per session, so simply dumping the beans into a colander and stirring or tossing them is sufficient cooling procedure. This process needs to take place over a sink or out-of-doors, so that the roasting chaff that floats free of the beans will not litter the counter or stove top.

If you own a kitchen range with an exhaust fan built into the stove top, the kind that evacuates kitchen odors downward rather than upward, you are in great luck. Simply place the colander full of hot beans over the exhaust fan and swirl or toss them. They will be warm to the touch within a minute or two.

You also can initiate the cooling process by *water quenching*, just as professional roasters often do. A pump spray dispenser, the kind with a trigger and a nozzle that adjusts to a fine mist (illustrated above), works very well. Simply fill the dispenser with distilled or filtered water, and while stirring or tossing the hot beans subject them to a few seconds of light, intermittent mist. You must perform this procedure *immediately* after roasting, and you must be careful not to overdo the application of water by spraying too long or using too coarse a spray. Complete instructions for water quenching are given on pages 169–171.

Why water quench? There are two reasons. If you roast a half-pound or more of coffee at a time you probably should water quench to hasten the cooling process, since the more coffee you roast the more slowly it cools. Second, I find that coffee water quenched with care and restraint tastes better than coffee that has been cooled simply by stirring or tossing. It seems to retain more aroma and brightness. The only reason I don't categorically recommend water quenching for all home roasting is that, done carelessly with a heavy hand, it can harm coffee and cause it to stale quickly. So if you do water quench, follow the instructions on pages 169–171 with care and sensitivity.

But again, don't be intimidated. Water quenching, like all home coffee-roasting procedures, only sounds difficult because we weren't raised doing it. After a few tries it becomes as easy and habitual as any other kitchen process.

Getting Out the Chaff

Chaff is paperlike stuff that appears as though by magic during roasting, apparently materializing straight out of the roasting beans. In fact these little brown flakes are fragments of the innermost skin (the silverskin) of the coffee fruit that still cling to the beans after processing has been completed. Roasting causes these bits of skin to lift off the bean.

The chaff presents contrasting issues depending on which roasting method you use.

With hot-air corn poppers or home fluid-bed roasters the chaff will be blown free of the seething beans during roasting, creating one kind of problem: how to keep it from wafting around the kitchen and landing on the counter or in the soup. Solutions for this problem appear with the roasting instructions following this chapter.

On the other hand, if you are using any other home-roasting method the chaff will remain mixed with the beans, presenting the problem of getting it out.

Fortunately, the same tossing or stirring process that facilitates cooling will rid the beans of most of their chaff. Any amount that is left in the beans will have little to no effect on flavor. Only in very large amounts can chaff be detected at all, then only as a slight muting or dulling of flavor. In fact, probably the single most important piece of advice to home roasters in regard to chaff is not to become obsessive about it.

However, advice for dealing with the occasional stubbornly chaff-retentive coffee is given on page 171.

Two Ways of Looking at Roasting Smoke

Finally there is the roasting smoke. The good news is it smells wonderful while you're roasting. To some people it still smells wonderful two hours later, but to many of us it becomes stale and cloying.

Furthermore, if you bring a coffee to a very dark roast and fail to vent the smoke, you may find yourself startled by the sudden screech of the smoke alarm, ruining both your nerves and the roasting beans, which you doubtless will abandon to their smoky fate as you scurry about opening windows and turning on fans.

Those who prefer light- to medium-roast styles will have less to be concerned about than those who like darker roasts, since beans produce their most voluminous and intense smoke as they are carried to darker styles. For example, bringing a few ounces of beans to a medium roast will produce very little smoke, whereas bringing ten ounces to a dark roast almost certainly will require aggressive venting to keep the smoke alarm quiet.

Fortunately, most contemporary kitchens are equipped with exhaust fans. Simply wait until the smoke begins to appear and turn on the fan. Failing an exhaust fan there is always the option of opening a window or door for a few minutes.

Keeping roasting chambers clean of residue also helps minimize the production of smoke.

Portable apparatus like fluid-bed roasters and hot-air poppers can be carried out to a porch or balcony in clement weather, much as Eduardo De Filippo's Neapolitans did with their *abbrustulaturi*. Don't try to operate fluid-bed apparatus outside in temperatures under 50°F/10°C however, since the cold may prevent them from achieving effective roast temperatures. In colder weather you have no choice but to set up these devices inside under a kitchen exhaust fan or next to a partly open window.

With stove-top roasting or with countertop convection ovens you also need either a good kitchen exhaust fan or a partly open window. Ovens that are components of kitchen ranges and built-in convection ovens typically are well-vented and carry the smoke outside.

After-Roast Resting

Resting doesn't refer to what you do to yourself after several minutes of vigilant home roasting, but what you do to the coffee. Freshly roasted beans are at their best anywhere from four hours to a day after roasting, when the bean chemistry has begun to stabilize.

Coffee fresh out of the roaster is still superb, however, so don't deprive yourself of enjoying it owing to gourmet obsessiveness. Just-roasted coffee may display somewhat less body and acidity than coffee that has been rested for a few hours, but it also resonates on the back of the palate with an almost uncannily long, rich finish.

Systematic Roasting: Controlling Variables

Some people simply toss some green coffee into whatever they're using for a roasting chamber, keep an eye on it, and when it's about the right color dump it and enjoy it. For most home roasters this off-hand approach produces excellent results.

Others relish the challenge of system and precision. A methodical approach is definitely the best way to achieve intimate knowledge of roast and coffee taste.

Informative experiment depends on control of four roasting variables:

- The amount of coffee roasted.

- The temperature inside the roasting chamber.

- The identity of the green coffee (in particular its approximate moisture content, largely a condition of age).

- The time or length of the roast.

Of course this list of variables assumes that you are using the *same* roasting method or technology (i.e., gas oven, hot-air corn popper, or other) for all of your experiments. The taste of a given roast style achieved by different methods will vary, sometimes greatly.

Like any good investigator, you need to control three of the four variables while systematically varying the fourth, meanwhile keeping careful record of the results. A sample log for recording notes on your roasting experiments appears on pages 146–149.

The two variables with which you are most likely to experiment are the identity of the green coffee and the length of time the roast is sustained. In other words, if you want to find out how two green coffees or blends of green coffees compare when brought to roughly the same style of roast, you should alter the identity of the coffees themselves while keeping constant the other three variables, including elapsed time of roast. On the other hand, if you are interested in how a single given coffee tastes at different styles or degrees of roast, obviously you should use the same green coffee or blend of coffees but increase the length of time you sustain the roast in regular, recorded increments.

The Four Variables in Detail

Here is a closer look at the four variables, again assuming that the method or equipment you are using for your experiments remains constant.

Amount of coffee you roast. The more coffee you roast the slower the beans respond to heat, so if you vary the amount of coffee you roast from session to session you will be prevented from making any meaningful connection between how long you have roasted a coffee and how it ends up looking and tasting. Fluid-bed roasters and hot-air corn poppers are particularly demanding in regard to how much coffee you roast, since they will not operate properly without the correct weight of beans to balance the upward thrust of the hot air. With oven and stove-top methods consistency in amount of coffee roasted per session is less important, particularly if you're the impulsive type who simply "roasts them until they're brown." But anyone carrying on systematic experiments should control this variable carefully.

Measuring green beans by weight on a kitchen food scale is more reliable than measuring them by volume, since beans differ in density. However, volume will work well enough in most home-roasting contexts.

Temperature inside the roasting chamber. For professional roasters who attempt to subtly influence the flavor profile of the coffee during roasting this is the most important variable of all. Unfortunately the simple technology available to home roasters makes sophisticated control of roasting-chamber temperature difficult, if not impossible.

With most home-roasting equipment you have no choice about roast-chamber temperature. With hot-air corn poppers and fluid-bed roasters the temperature is built in. Stove-top roasting allows a very rough control. With convection ovens you can change temperature settings, but usually the only practical setting for coffee roasting is the highest available, so the question is moot. Only gas-oven roasting allows you to control roast-chamber temperature deliberately and measurably.

Consequently, the best approach for most home-roasting methods is to maintain the same temperature throughout your sessions and influence style or degree of roast simply by varying the length of time you keep the beans in the roasting chamber. If your method allows you a choice of roast temperature (essentially, if you are using either a gas oven or a stove-top roaster fitted with candy thermometer), start with a temperature of about 500°F/260°C. (The exception is the Palani Plantation roaster; when using the Palani pan start with a temperature of 425°F/220°C.) If you have to wait longer than eight or ten minutes for the onset of pyrolysis, signaled by coffee-smelling smoke and crackling sounds, raise the temperature to 520°F/270°C (or 450°F/235°C with the Palani pan) and try again. On the other hand, if pyrolysis sets in sooner than four minutes into the roast, lower your beginning temperature to about 475°F/245°C for your next session. Unless instructions indicate otherwise, *never attempt to roast coffee at temperatures lower than about 460°F/240°C. With stove-top poppers, never go higher than 520°F/270°C; with gas ovens never higher than about 550°F/290°C.* Once you settle on a workable temperature, which induces pyrolysis in less than eight or ten minutes but no sooner than three or four, stay with it until you learn a bit about the roasting process.

At that point, if you are using a gas oven or stove-top popper with thermometer, you may wish to begin experimenting with roast-chamber temperature in order to compensate for differences among green beans or to influence taste. See the detailed instructions for those methods following this chapter.

Identity of the green coffee.   Green beans all roast slightly differently; some roast *very* differently. If you are carrying out systematic experiments to learn about roast taste or how a given coffee responds when brought to a variety of roast styles, control this variable by using the same crop or blend of green beans for every session in your series of experiments.

The moister and denser the bean, the slower it roasts and the higher the temperatures it will absorb on the way to the same roast style. Professional roasters often measure bean density and adjust roast-chamber temperatures accordingly. More intuitive professionals may compensate for differences among green coffees by regulating roast temperatures, based on their experience with a particular coffee and their knowledge of its age.

Most home roasters can do neither, since the majority of home-roasting methods don't allow us to make adjustments to roast-chamber temperature for any reason. (Again, the limited exceptions are gas-oven and stove-top corn-popper roasting; see the instructions for those methods in the section following this chapter.) All we can do is be aware of differences in how quickly a given coffee may roast, and make very rough corresponding adjustments in our procedure. The following generalizations may be helpful, although probably only the last point, concerning decaffeinated beans, is significant in the context of home roasting.

- Fresh beans less than a year old (*new crop*) from high growing areas (the best Guatemalan, Costa Rican, and Colombian coffees, in particular) tend to be hard and moist, and may roast relatively slowly.

- Older beans (a year or more since processing, called *past crop* or *old crop*, plus deliberately aged coffees) and beans from lower growing areas may roast slightly faster than newer-crop, higher-grown coffees, although for most home roasters this small distinction will be irrelevant.

- Decaffeinated coffees are *very* sensitive, however, and typically roast dramatically faster (15 to 25 percent) than fresh hard-bean coffees. With decaffeinated beans you should be prepared from the first sign of roasting smoke and crackling to check the appearance of the beans obsessively and dump them for cooling with decision.

Time or duration of the roast. This is the most easily controlled and most important variable in home roasting. If you carefully control the other three variables and use the same roasting method from session to session, you should be able to correlate the time of the roast fairly accurately with the final color, style, and taste of the roasted beans. You can't achieve absolute consistency, since ambient temperature and atmospheric pressure both affect roasting time, but you can come close.

Record Keeping

Take a look at the sample roasting log on the following pages. Don't be intimidated by the number of columns or headings; several can be ignored by all but the most dedicated home roaster. Note that if you are consistent from session to session with roast-chamber temperature, quantity of coffee roasted, and quench method you can obtain useful results by recording only five to six columns: the identity of the green coffee, the date of the roast, the final bean temperature (if your method permits), the elapsed time of the roast, the appearance of the roasted beans, and your tasting notes.

You may not know or care about the age of the beans. The temperature in the roasting chamber may not be measurable, or you may choose never to vary it once you start your experiments. Pyrolysis or first crack may occur at about the same time during the roast if you are using a consistent method and roast-chamber temperature.

For advice on systematically tasting coffee see the list of tasting terms on pages 58–61 and the Afterword on cupping on pages 186–192.

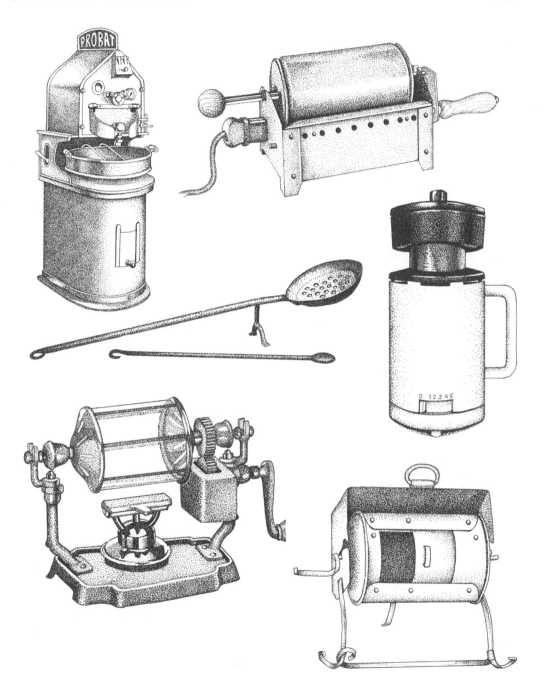

Sample Home-Roasting Log

Note that "roast 'em till they're brown" improvisors don't need to fool with charts like this one. Also note that not all columns are relevant to all roasting methods; fill in the columns that tell you what you need to know. Finally, be prepared to accept the fact that no matter how

NAME OF COFFEE	APPROXIMATE AGE OF COFFEE	DATE OF ROAST	WEIGHT OR VOLUME OF BEANS ROASTED	ROAST-CHAMBER TEMPERATURE (if measurable and variable)	MINUTES TO ONSET OF PYROLYSIS ("first crack")

Example (assumes stove-top roasting using Theater II corn popper with candy thermometer installed to monitor temperature in roast chamber):

NAME OF COFFEE	APPROXIMATE AGE OF COFFEE	DATE OF ROAST	WEIGHT OR VOLUME OF BEANS ROASTED	ROAST-CHAMBER TEMPERATURE	MINUTES TO ONSET OF PYROLYSIS
Kenyan AA	New crop (less than a year)	6/3/95	8 ounces by weight	500°F/260°C	5 minutes

Example (assumes hot-air popper with candy thermometer installed to monitor bean temperature):

Brazilian Santos	Old crop	6/3/95	4 ounces by volume	NA	4 minutes

Example (assumes gas-oven roasting):

Sumatran Mandheling	Old crop. Aged? (Brownish beans)	6/3/95	11 ounces by weight	520°F/270°C	14 minutes

consistent you are, roasts still will differ from session to session. Home-roasting methods are still too offhand to permit systematic compensation for subtleties like changes in atmospheric pressure and variations in green-bean density. Tasting and making observations about surface oils are activities ideally carried out the day following the roast. The examples are meant to suggest how the form might be used.

FINAL BEAN TEMPERATURE (if measurable)	ELAPSED TIME OF ROAST	QUENCH METHOD	ROAST CATEGORY & APPEARANCE (approximate color or roast name: dry/oily surface; uniform/non-uniform beans)	MISCELLANEOUS NOTES	TASTING NOTES (acidity, body, taste, aroma, complexity; for dark roasts sweetness, pungency; or use tasting charts, pages 191–192)
NA	8 minutes	Water	Medium brown; some scorched beans	Lazy turning at beginning of roast.	Superb Kenya taste; explosive acidity. Scorched beans didn't seem to matter.
450°F/230°C	9 minutes	Air	Moderately dark brown; "espresso roast." Patches of oil on surface.		Nice espresso; rich, complex, low-toned; no acidity. Heavy body but maybe too mellow for me.
NA	19 minutes	Water	Medium brown; some slightly scorched beans, uneven roasting.	Used cookie-sheet diverter; start with higher temperature setting next time.	Sumatra character came through; rich, deep body; complex. Maybe lost some acidity by long roast.

Home-Roasting Log

NAME OF COFFEE	APPROXIMATE AGE OF COFFEE	DATE OF ROAST	WEIGHT OR VOLUME OF BEANS ROASTED	ROAST-CHAMBER TEMPERATURE (if measurable and variable)	MINUTES TO ONSET OF PYROLYSIS ("first crack")

<u>FINAL BEAN TEMPERATURE</u> (if measurable)	<u>ELAPSED TIME OF ROAST</u>	<u>QUENCH METHOD</u>	<u>ROAST CATEGORY & APPEARANCE</u> (approximate color or roast name: dry/oily surface; uniform/non-uniform beans)	<u>MISCELLANEOUS NOTES</u>	<u>TASTING NOTES</u> (acidity, body, taste, aroma, complexity; for dark roasts sweetness, pungency; or use tasting charts, pages 191–192)

Quick Guide to Home-Roasting Procedure

Here are instructions for five home-roasting methods. Near the end of this section you will find directions for two optional procedures: water quenching (accelerating cooling of hot beans with a fine spray of water) and winnowing (separating chaff from roasted beans). A brief note about roasting decaffeinated and other specially handled coffee concludes the section.

For background and overview on these five methods and their associated processes see Chapter 5.

Stove-Top Roasting with a Crank-Type Corn Popper

Advantages
— Beans are accessible and can be studied easily as roast progresses.
— Beans roast more uniformly than with oven method.
— More beans can be roasted per session than with fluid-bed method.
— Effective for all roast styles, including very dark.

Disadvantages
— Beans roast slightly less uniformly than with fluid-bed method.
— Temperature cannot be controlled with precision.
— Process requires continuous cranking and attention during roast session.
— Corn popper requires simple modification before it can be used for coffee roasting.

Taste Notes

— Performed carefully, roasting with a stove-top corn popper produces a balanced, classic-tasting roast with more body and complexity but possibly less acidity and aroma than fluid-bed roasts.

What You Need

For roasting sessions:

— Felknor International Theater II or similar stove-top corn popper (6-quart model) modified to accommodate candy thermometer as described below.

— Sample beans roasted to style you prefer.

— Green beans (approximately 9 ounces by weight or 12 fluid ounces per session for Felknor 6-quart model).

— Colander for cooling, large enough to accommodate about twice the volume of green beans you intend to roast.

— Kitchen exhaust fan or open window to dissipate roasting smoke.

— Oven mitt.

For modifications to popper:

— Candy/deep-fry thermometer with dial and metal shaft that measures temperatures to 400°F/200°C or higher. Cooper, Springfield, UEI model T550, or Taylor brands all work well.

— Metal nuts or washers with holes large enough to slide onto shaft of thermometer and with sufficient total thickness to occupy about $\frac{1}{2}$ to 1 inch of shaft length. (Not needed with UEI model T550 or other thermometers with shafts 5 or fewer inches long.)

— $\frac{1}{4}$ inch high-speed drill bit and drill.

Procedure

Modification to Theater II corn popper (see illustrations, pages 123 and 152):

— Drill $\frac{1}{4}$ inch hole through popper lid. Lid has two hinged halves. Drill hole through center of half-lid that has clamp closure and words "Theater II" stamped on it. (Position hole about at base of second "t" in "Theater.") Carefully remove and dispose of all aluminum shavings.

— Remove clip from thermometer. String sufficient metal nuts and/or washers on upper part of thermometer shaft to raise tip of thermometer about $\frac{5}{8}$ to $\frac{3}{4}$ inch above bottom surface of popper.

— Insert thermometer in popper with nuts and washers positioned between bottom of dial and upper surface of lid.
— Reach inside popper and slip clip back onto shaft of thermometer. Slide clip up to underside of lid to secure thermometer in place. (UEI model 550 has a short shaft so requires no nuts or washers. It lacks a clip, and simply rests loosely in hole. It may rattle around, but will be perfectly functional.)

Roasting procedure:
— Cautions:
  — *Never use high heat under popper. On electric stoves start with larger burner set to medium; on gas stoves start with low flame.*
  — *Never use popper without thermometer installed.*
  — *Never leave popper unattended over heat.*
— Place sample roasted beans where they can be easily seen for color comparison to beans inside popper. Make certain cooling colander and oven mitt are at hand. If you wish to accelerate cooling of beans by water quenching (see pages 169–171), have pump spray bottle ready.
— Preheat popper by placing over medium setting (electric range) or low flame (gas range). Stand by and observe thermometer dial. Temperature will climb fairly rapidly. When indicator passes 400°F/200°C carefully modulate heat setting until temperature steadies at approximately 475°F/240°C to 500°F/260°C. (Candy thermometer may be calibrated only to 400°F/200°C. If so, thermometer still can be used to accurately approximate higher readings. For example, 500°F/260°C is achieved when pointer circles past 400°F/200°C and returns to 100°F/40°C; 450°F/230°C is halfway between the two, and so on.) *Make note of burner setting.* If you have a gas range, indicate approximate setting with marking pen or bit of tape. Use this setting for future roasting sessions.
— Place green beans in popper. Close lid.
— Begin cranking handle of popper. You don't need to crank rapidly, and you can step away, but you must persist. Abandoning cranking for more than a minute will certainly cause bottom layer of beans to scorch. Occasionally beans may catch between stirring rod and bottom of popper, causing crank to resist turning. If so, simply reverse direction of cranking. If crank still resists, see "Problems and Refinements," page 153.

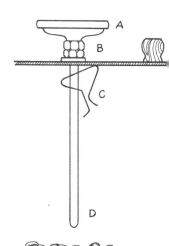

Correct installation of candy/deep-fry thermometer in the Felknor Theater II stove-top corn popper. The thermometer enables the home roaster to monitor temperature inside the popper before and during the roast. See page 123 for an overview illustration of the popper with thermometer installed.
(A) Thermometer dial.
(B) Nuts and/or washers sufficient to raise the tip of the thermometer about ⅝ to ¾ inches above the inside bottom surface of popper.
(C) Thermometer clip flush to the bottom surface of popper lid to secure the thermometer in place.
(D) Tip of thermometer raised just high enough to clear stirring rods and roasting beans.

— After beans are in popper, temperature as indicated by thermometer will gradually decrease. If temperature declines below 325°F/165°C, turn up heat slightly.

— During remainder of session thermometer will register slowly recovering temperatures, typically stabilizing at 350°F/175°C to 375°F/190°C. (Actual roasting temperatures on bottom of popper are higher.)

— Soon after coffee-smelling roasting smoke appears and crackling sounds set in (usually in 4 to 7 minutes), start kitchen exhaust fan to ventilate smoke.

— About 1 minute after smoke and crackling begin (for lighter roasts) to 2 minutes (for darker roasts), check beans by lifting free half of popper cover. Compare color of roasting beans with color of sample beans.

— Repeat visual checking process at about 1-minute intervals until beans reach same color as your sample or slightly lighter. Immediately turn off heat and dump beans into colander.

— Over sink or out-of-doors, stir or toss beans in colander until cool enough to touch and until most loose roasting chaff has floated free. To accelerate cooling, water quench as described on pages 169–171. For more on chaff removal, see page 171.

Problems and Refinements

— If crank resists turning, heat may be causing bottom of popper to expand upward, interfering with movement of shaft that turns wire stirring vanes. Simply wait until popper is cool and place tip of kitchen spoon or similar long, blunt tool against bottom of popper next to shaft and press down firmly. Repeat on opposite side of shaft. Bottom of popper will depress slightly and (usually) permanently, freeing shaft to turn without interference. If your efforts produce slight indentations in bottom of popper, don't be concerned; operation will still be a success.

— Roasting times can be accelerated by cautiously raising heat setting on stove after crackling and smoke indicate pyrolysis has begun. (Do not *start* with temperatures higher than 500°F/260°C, however.)

— Raising heat after onset of pyrolysis will produce more acidy medium roasts and more pungent dark roasts. Keep in mind, however, that roast develops quickly at higher temperatures, and intensified roasting smoke may make observing bean color inside popper difficult.

Roasting with Recommended Designs of Hot-Air Corn Popper

Advantages

— Somewhat simpler than other methods. Roasting temperature, for example, is already established.
— Produces more consistent and uniform roast than other methods.

Disadvantages

— Only units with recommended popping-chamber design (see illustration below) should be used to roast coffee. Other designs are not suitable for that purpose.
— Roasts considerably less coffee per session than stove-top and oven methods.
— Roasting smoke tends to be more difficult to control and vent than with oven methods.
— Regular use to achieve very dark roasts (black-brown and shiny with oil, common names *Italian* or *dark French*) will shorten life of popper. However, can be used to produce moderately dark to dark roasts, usually called French or espresso. See Quick Reference Guide to Roast Styles, pages 68–69.

Taste Notes

— Hot-air poppers roast relatively quickly, thereby emphasizing bright, acidy notes in medium roasts and pungency in dark roasts. Taste tends to be clean and straightforward compared to more complex taste of beans roasted in gas oven or stove-top corn popper.

Interiors of popping chambers in three typical hot-air corn poppers. *Use only designs like the one on the right for coffee roasting,* in which hot air issues into the chamber from diagonal slots in the chamber wall. *Do not use designs like those pictured in center and on left,* in which hot air issues into the popping chamber from the bottom of the chamber.

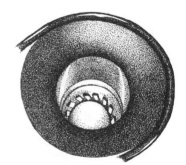

What You Need

— Hot-air popper of recommended design only (see illustration on page 154). Other designs are not suitable for coffee roasting.
— Large bowl to collect chaff.
— Sample beans roasted to style you prefer.
— Green beans (same volume per session as volume of popping corn recommended by manufacturer of popper, usually about 4 fluid ounces or ½ cup).
— Colander for cooling, large enough to accommodate about twice the volume of green beans you intend to roast.
— 2 oven mitts or pot holders.

A hot-air corn popper with bowl positioned to catch roasting chaff as it drifts out of the popper.

Procedure

— Position popper under kitchen exhaust fan or near open window to dissipate roasting smoke. Can be positioned out-of-doors, but only in clement weather; low ambient temperatures (under 50°F/ 10°C) may prevent coffee from roasting properly.
— Place in popping chamber same volume of green beans as volume of popping corn recommended in instructions accompanying popper. *Do not exceed this volume.*
— Make certain plastic chute (hoodlike component over popping chamber) and butter cup (cup that sits in hood over popping chamber) are in place. Do not operate without chute and butter cup; they assist in maintaining proper temperature in popping/roasting chamber.
— Place large bowl under chute opening to catch chaff (see illustration on left).
— Place sample roasted beans where they can be easily seen for color comparison to beans inside popper. Make certain cooling colander and oven mitts are at hand. If you wish to accelerate cooling of beans by water quenching (see pages 169–171), have pump spray bottle ready.
— Plug in or turn on popper.
— In approximately 3 or 4 minutes dark, coffee-smelling smoke will appear and beans will begin to crackle. Turn on kitchen exhaust fan if indoors.
— About 1 minute (for light to medium roasts) to 3 minutes (for moderately dark to dark roasts) after smoke appears and crack-

ling sets in, begin checking color of beans by lifting out butter cup with oven mitt and peeking into popping chamber.

— Continue checking color of roasting beans against color of sample beans at 30-second to 1-minute intervals.

— *Roast develops relatively quickly with hot-air poppers:* typically 5 to 6 minutes to medium roast, 7 to 8 minutes to medium dark, 9 to dark.

— When roasting beans are the same color or slightly lighter than sample beans, *unplug or turn off popper* and, *using oven mitts,* immediately lift popper and pour beans out of popping chamber through chute opening into cooling colander.

— Carry colander outside or place under kitchen exhaust fan and stir or toss beans until warm to touch. To accelerate cooling, water quench as described on pages 169–171.

Problems and Refinements

— Hot-air poppers incorporate safety switches to prevent overheating. Continuous roasting sessions may trigger switch, causing popper to shut down temporarily. Simply allow popper to cool, then resume roasting.

— Hot-air poppers can be easily fitted with metal candy thermometers to monitor approximate inner temperature of roasting beans. Since internal temperature of beans correlates to color or style of roast, this modification permits emulation of procedure of technically inclined professionals who use approximate internal temperature of beans to determine when to conclude roasting session.

    This modification differs in purpose from the somewhat similar procedure suggested for Felknor stove-top popper earlier in section. Here the goal is to monitor temperature of roasting beans, not air temperature.

What you need for modification

— Candy thermometer with dial and metal shaft that measures temperatures at least to 400°F/200°C. Shaft must be long enough to project from bottom of plastic butter cup to a point about 1 to 3 inches above bottom of popping/roasting chamber. Cooper-brand thermometer fits most poppers perfectly. Taylor brand has shaft about ¹/₂ inch longer than Cooper; Insta-Read is longer still. Shaft of UEI T550 may be too short for most popper models.

Hot-air popper with candy/deep-fry thermometer installed in butter cup. The thermometer measures the approximate internal heat of the roasting beans, permitting monitoring of the progress of the roast by temperature.

— ¹/₄ inch high-speed drill bit and drill.
— If necessary: metal nuts or washers with holes large enough to slide onto shaft of thermometer. These may be required as spacers between underside of thermometer dial and top surface of butter cup to raise tip of thermometer shaft to recommended minimum 1 inch from bottom of popping/roasting chamber.

Modification procedure
(see illustrations below and page 156):
— Drill ¹/₄ inch hole through center of plastic butter cup. Carefully remove and dispose of all plastic shavings.
— Remove clip from thermometer. If necessary, string sufficient metal nuts and/or washers on upper part of thermometer shaft to raise tip of thermometer a minimum of approximately 1 inch above bottom of popping/roasting chamber.
— Insert thermometer in popper with nuts and washers (if necessary) positioned between underside of dial and upper surface of butter cup.
— Slip clip back onto shaft of thermometer. Slide clip up to underside of butter cup to secure thermometer in place.

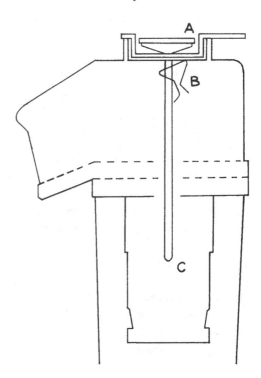

Installation of a candy/ deep-fry thermometer in the recommended design of hot-air popper. Use recommended design popper only (see page 154). The thermometer permits monitoring the approximate internal temperature of the beans as they roast. (A) Thermometer dial. (B) Themometer clip flush to the bottom surface of the butter cup to secure the thermometer in place. (C) Thermometer tip protruding to within 1 to 3 inches of the bottom surface of popping/roasting chamber. The green beans may not touch the thermometer tip at the start of roasting but will expand and surround it as roasting proceeds. (If the thermometer tip extends to closer than 1 inch from the bottom of the popping chamber, insert sufficient nuts or washers between the underside of the thermometer dial and the surface of the butter cup to raise the tip to a minimum 1 inch above the bottom.)

Monitoring progress of roast with installed thermometer:
— Consult Quick Reference Guide to Roast Styles on pages 68–69
for equivalences of bean temperature and roast style.
— When temperature on thermometer approximately matches temperature for roast style you prefer, *unplug or turn off popper* and,
using oven mitts, immediately remove plastic chute together
with butter cup and thermometer from top of popper, lift popper,
and pour beans into cooling colander.
— Candy thermometer may be calibrated only to 400°F/200°C. If
so, thermometer still can be used to approximate higher temperature readings accurately. For example, 450°F/230°C is
achieved when pointer has circled completely around dial and
is centered between 400°F and 100°F (200°C and 40°C).
— Regular production of roasts with final internal temperatures
higher than about 460°F/240°C (color dark to very dark brown;
common names Italian, dark French) may significantly shorten
life of hot-air poppers.

Roasting with a Home Fluid-Bed Roaster

As I write, inexpensive fluid-bed devices designed specifically for
home coffee roasting are slowly making their way to market through
thickets of patent issues and investor anxiety. I do not expect any to
appear on the shelves until 1997. Until then, the only home fluid-bed
roasting devices generally available are modifications of other products: a hot-air corn popper and a heat gun, both redesigned for coffee
roasting by Michael Sivetz. A third, the Sirocco, was intended from the
start for home roasting, but is no longer manufactured. Only a few units
remain available at a high price and in odd foreign voltages. For ordering information for the Sivetz and Sirocco units, see Resources.

Both the Sirocco and the Sivetz converted corn popper produce
excellent results, but given their high price I find it difficult to recommend them in preference to an ordinary, unconverted corn popper.
Their main advantages are their somewhat larger bean capacities and
the convenience of their built-in cooling cycles: Rather than unplugging the unit and manually lifting it to dump the beans into a colander for cooling, you either flip a switch (Sivetz modified corn popper)
or allow a mechanical timer to flip a switch for you (Sirocco).

Potential new roasters, the Sivetz modified corn popper, and the
Sirocco all resemble one another in general design and operating
principles, differing only in detail. The instructions that follow make

reference to the Sivetz modified corn popper and the Sirocco roaster but will be helpful with all home fluid-bed devices, including those that may reach the shelves in the near future.

Advantages

— Somewhat simpler than other methods. Roasting temperature, for example, is already established.
— Produce more consistent and uniform roast than oven and stove-top methods.
— Better models (including currently available Sivetz modified corn popper, Sirocco roasters, and anticipated new machines) have a cool-down cycle, simplifying cooling beans after roasting.
— Some models (including Sirocco and anticipated new machines) permit easy visual monitoring of roasting beans.
— Currently available Sivetz modified corn popper incorporates a high-temperature candy thermometer that acts as a heat probe, making monitoring roast easy and relatively precise.
— Sporadically available Sirocco model and anticipated new machines incorporate a timer that permits running unit unattended.
— Sporadically available Sirocco model and anticipated new machines incorporate chaff-collecting mechanisms. Sirocco uses paper filters to moderately reduce emission of roasting smoke.

Disadvantages

— Roast considerably less coffee per session than stove-top or oven methods.
— Currently available models must be ordered by mail and are considerably more expensive than ad hoc equipment used in other home roasting methods. Anticipated new fluid-bed roasters will retail for considerably less than currently available fluid-bed units, but almost certainly will cost more than hot-air corn poppers.
— Sivetz modified corn popper does not incorporate effective chaff collector; much of chaff blows out top of device.
— Sivetz device cannot be used on a regular basis to produce very dark (dark French or Italian) roast styles.
— Sirocco roaster requires ongoing purchase of paper filters.

Taste Notes

— Currently available models roast relatively quickly, thereby emphasizing bright, acidy notes in medium styles and pungency in darker styles. Taste tends to be clean and straightforward compared to more complex taste of beans roasted in gas oven and stove-top corn popper.

What You Need

— Fluid-bed roasting device and accompanying instructions; see Resources for purchase information.
— Green beans (see instructions accompanying roaster).
— Sample beans roasted to style you prefer (optional with Sivetz modified corn popper).

Procedure

Fluid-bed devices may differ in details of operation. Follow instructions that come with device carefully. The following points may be helpful. For instructions on visual monitoring of roasting beans, consult Procedure under Roasting with Recommended Designs of Hot-Air Corn Popper, pages 155–156.

— Always use recommended weight or volume of green coffee beans. Too few beans will bounce inside chamber; too many will not agitate properly. In either case taste will be adversely affected.
— Sirocco and anticipated new machines incorporate spring-loaded, mechanical timers that initiate the cooling cycle automatically after a preset number of minutes. Instructions accompanying the unit will tell you to set timer at various positions for lighter, medium, or darker roasts. These settings are only approximate, however. The precise degree of roast will vary depending on identity of green beans and ambient temperature. Either experiment with various settings until you achieve the roast style you desire for a given supply of green beans, or monitor roasting beans visually, and when beans have achieved color you are aiming for, manually advance timer to cooling position. For more on visual monitoring of roasting beans with fluid-bed roasting machines and corn poppers, see pages 155-156. Be particularly attentive when roasting decaffeinated beans, which may develop to a given roast style considerably more quickly than untreated beans.

— Roast will develop relatively quickly. *Remain attentive; do not abandon device while roast is in progress* unless it incorporates a timer that automatically triggers cooling cycle.

— When producing darker roasts, vent smoke by using unit out-of-doors, near an open window, or under a kitchen exhaust fan. Do not attempt to roast out-of-doors in temperatures below 50°F/10°C, however, since ambient temperature may prevent unit from generating sufficient heat.

— With Sivetz unit, operate out-of-doors in clement weather or in garage or workroom, since chaff will blow out of top of device and settle on indoor surfaces.

— Sivetz modified corn popper permits monitoring progress of roast by means of a metal candy thermometer. Tip of thermometer protrudes into mass of roasting beans, roughly measuring their internal temperature. Since internal temperature of beans correlates to degree or style of roast, Sivetz device permits emulation of procedure of professionals who often use approximate internal temperature of beans to determine when to conclude roasting session.

— Consult Quick Reference Guide to Roast Styles on pages 68–69 or instructions accompanying Sivetz unit for equivalences of bean temperature and roast style. When temperature on thermometer approximately matches temperature for roast style you prefer, activate cooling cycle by tripping switch as indicated in instructions.

— Monitoring of roast also can be performed visually, as described in procedures for other roasting methods.

Roasting in a Gas Oven

Advantages
— Temperature in roasting chamber (i.e., oven) is easily controlled and repeatable.

— With most gas ovens roasting smoke is effectively vented.

— More coffee can be roasted in given session than with other methods.

— Control over temperature enables those who experiment to roughly compensate for differences in density of green beans and broadly influence taste of roast.

Disadvantages
— Hot spots inside some ovens and lack of strong convection currents may cause beans to roast unevenly: some beans lighter,

some darker, some in between. Solutions to this problem may
require patience and experiment.
— Timing roast can be difficult because color of beans may not be
uniform and beans may be difficult to see inside oven.
— Precision in roast style may be difficult to attain owing to
uneven roasting.

Taste Notes

— Somewhat uneven roast brings out complexity and depth of
taste, since a range of roast styles may be present simultaneously in any given sample of beans. Gas-oven roasting probably
produces best results for those who like medium dark through
moderately dark (espresso) styles. It probably should be
avoided by those who prefer either light or very dark roasts.

What You Need

— Ordinary kitchen gas oven. (*Do not attempt to use microwave
ovens for coffee roasting.* Conventional electric kitchen ovens
can be used with the following instructions, but typically produce roasts too uneven for most tastes. For electric convection
ovens consult pages 166–169.)
— One or more flat, perforated baking pans with raised edges.
Palani Plantation produces inexpensive foil pans especially
designed for oven coffee-roasting (see Resources). Some baking
pans designed to crisp bottom crusts of bread or pizza also work

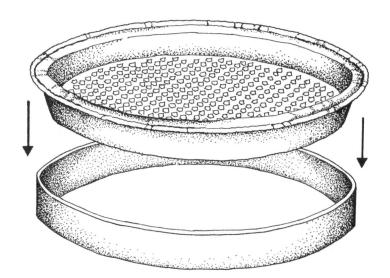

The Palani Plantation
roasting pan ensemble.
The foil pan drops
inside an aluminum
ring. The ring channels
and intensifies the mild
oven convection cur-
rents that help achieve
an even roast in gas
ovens.

A good perforated pan for gas-oven and convection-oven roasting, the Mirro Crispi Crust baking pan.

well. Perforations should be relatively close together (no more than ¹/₈ inch apart) and small enough to prevent coffee beans from falling through (maximum about ³/₁₆-inch diameter). Pan should have raised lip around edges. See illustrated examples of such pans above and on pages 164 and 167, and suggestions for obtaining them in Resources. In larger ovens more than one baking pan can be used per roasting session. Palani Plantation pans roast about 4 ounces of beans per pan per session; recommended Mirro Crispi Crust pan (Mirro item #825) about 10 ounces per pan.

— Sample beans roasted to style you prefer.
— Enough green beans to uniformly cover surface of baking pan(s) one bean deep.
— Colander for cooling, large enough to accommodate about twice the volume of green beans you intend to roast.
— 2 oven mitts or pot holders.
— Flashlight (necessary only if interior of oven is not illuminated and remains dark when you peer through window or crack open door).

Procedure

— *Note:* Virtually all gas ovens will produce a reasonably consistent and very flavorful roast, but success may require patience and experiment. If your first roast emerges uneven in color, don't give up. Consult "Problems and Refinements" for this section.

— For Palani Plantation pan: Follow instructions accompanying
   pan. Preheat oven to 425°F/220°C to 450°F/230°C. For
   brighter, more acidy taste in medium roasts and more pungency
   in dark roasts try upper range of temperature; for more body
   and less acidity/pungency use lower end of range.
— For other pans: Preheat oven to 500°F/260°C to 540°F/280°C
   depending on condition of green coffee and desired taste characteristics. For fresh, new-crop coffees, set to 540°F/280°C; for
   past crop, aged, or monsooned beans, set to 520°F/270°C; for
   decaffeinated beans set to 500°F/260°C. For brighter, more
   acidy taste in medium roasts and more pungency in dark roasts
   try upper range of temperature; for more body and less acidity/
   pungency use lower end of range. If beans take longer than 15
   minutes to reach a medium roast or 20 minutes to reach a moderately dark to dark (espresso) roast, or if they taste bland or
   flat, start with higher temperature on subsequent sessions.
— Spread green beans *closely together, one bean deep* (no deeper)
   across *entire* perforated surface of baking pan. Pat beans down
   with flattened hand until they are densely but evenly distributed, touching or almost touching, but not piled atop one another.
   Make certain *all* of pan is covered with a single layer of beans.
   See illustration below.
— Place baking pan charged with beans on middle shelf of preheated oven.
— Place sample roasted beans where they can be easily seen for
   color comparison to beans inside oven. Make certain cooling

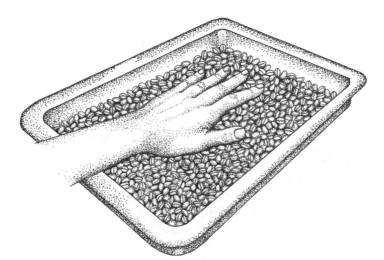

Patting the surface of
the green beans with
an open hand is a
good way to make cer-
tain the beans are dis-
tributed evenly, one
deep, across the entire
surface of the pan.

colander and oven mitts are at hand. If you wish to accelerate cooling of beans by water quenching (see pages 169–171), have pump spray bottle ready.

— In about 7 to 10 minutes you should hear crackling from inside oven and smell coffeelike scent of roasting smoke.

— About 2 minutes after crackling begins (for lighter roasts) to 3 minutes after it begins (for darker roasts) peek inside oven, with flashlight if necessary. If oven has no window, crack open oven door *only as long* as it takes to compare color of beans inside oven to sample of roasted beans.

— Continue peeking at about 1-minute intervals, making comparison to sample beans. When average color of roasting beans is approximately same as sample, pull baking pans out of oven, using oven mitts, and dump beans into colander.

— Over sink or out-of-doors, stir or toss beans in colander until cool enough to touch and until most loose roasting chaff has floated free. To accelerate cooling, water quench as described on pages 169–171. For more on chaff removal, see page 171.

Problems and Refinements

Actual temperatures in ovens may differ from control settings. Consider comparing actual temperature as indicated by an oven thermometer to control settings before first roasting session. Compensate for any difference when setting temperatures thereafter.

Beans always will roast somewhat unevenly. Nevertheless, they may taste as good as or better than uniformly roasted beans. Try them. If you don't like flavor complexity, or if range between dark and light beans is too great (if darkest beans are almost black and lightest beans medium-brown, for example), one or more of the following adjustments may be needed:

— Make certain beans are uniformly spread one bean deep but no more over *entire* surface of pan.

— Use middle shelf of oven. If results on middle shelf are unsatisfactory, experiment with higher or lower placement.

— Place one or more cookie sheets on lower shelf of oven to break up flow of hot air through oven and thus dissipate hot spots. Arrange pans charged with coffee beans on upper shelf above cookie sheets. Situate cookie sheets in relation to bean-charged pans so as to break up pattern of hot spots revealed by previous roast sessions. In other words, if beans in middle of roasting pan emerge darker than beans at sides, position cookie sheet directly below roasting pan. If darker beans are at back of pan, position cookie sheet somewhat farther back in oven than roasting pan, and so on.

If cookie-sheet strategy is successful (it usually is), beans may take longer to reach pyrolysis. If beans take longer than 15 minutes to reach a medium roast or 20 minutes to reach a moderately dark (espresso) roast, or if they taste bland or flat, start with higher temperature on subsequent sessions.

— If you are using more than one shelf in oven and beans roast unevenly from shelf to shelf, arrange pans on one shelf only (middle shelf is usually best).

— If cookie-sheet strategy fails and beans still roast unevenly across surface of pan, rotate pan about half a turn approximately every 3 minutes during roast. This is a last resort and seldom required.

Oven roasting offers potential for control over temperature and timing. Keep records of oven settings and elapsed time of roasts while roasting same amount of similar green beans. When you achieve a roast you enjoy, use same oven setting next time and set kitchen timer for 2 minutes or so before estimated termination of roast, thus minimizing time spent peeking into oven to check roast color. You still must make final decision when to stop roast based on visual observation of bean color, since differences in atmospheric pressure and ambient temperature alter length of a roast from session to session. See pages 146–149 for more advanced experiments with record keeping.

Roasting in a Convection Oven

Note: Only convection ovens with maximum settings of 450°F/230°C or higher can be used to roast coffee. Test oven for actual heat output. Preheat oven at maximum temperature setting (usually 450°F/230°C or 500°F/260°C) with oven thermometer positioned inside. If actual temperature inside oven as registered by thermometer peaks at 475°F/245°C to 500°F/260°C, oven will produce an acceptable to excellent roast. If actual temperature is 450°F/230°C to 460°F/240°C try a roast, but most likely beans will not expand and coffee will taste flat. If temperature registers under 450°F/230°C oven will be useless for coffee roasting.

Advantages

— Temperature in roasting chamber (i.e., oven) is easily controlled and repeatable.

— More coffee can be roasted in given session than with fluid-bed methods.

— Produces a relatively consistent and uniform roast.

— Most convection ovens permit easy visual inspection of roasting beans, making monitoring roast color easier than with other methods.

Disadvantage

— Maximum temperature in most convection ovens (see earlier note) is barely high enough to induce a proper roast.

Taste Notes

— *Important:* Most convection ovens produce a mild, sweet roast with muted acidity and relatively weak aroma.

What You Need

— Convection oven with maximum temperature of at least 450°F/230°C, preferably 500°F/260°C. (See earlier note. Do not purchase a convection oven for coffee roasting unless it offers a maximum temperature setting of at least 500°F/260°C and permits easy visual inspection of roasting beans through clear, nontinted glass.)

— Perforated baking pan of kind recommended for gas oven roasting (see below).

— Sample beans roasted to style you prefer.

— Enough green beans to uniformly cover surface of baking pan(s) one bean deep.

Details of two perforated baking pans or sheets appropriate for roasting coffee in a gas or convection oven. The important features for any oven coffee-roasting pan are holes sufficiently close together to permit circulation of hot air and small enough to prevent the beans from falling through or catching, and a raised lip around the edge of the pan.

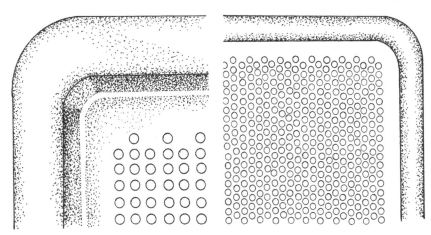

— Colander for cooling, large enough to accommodate about twice the volume of green beans you intend to roast.

— 2 oven mitts or pot holders.

Procedure

— Make certain raised rack or shelf is in place in oven. Do not place perforated baking pan directly on carousel or floor of oven. Use raised rack or shelf. *Do not use microwave or mixed microwave-convection function* in ovens that offer both convection and microwave options.

— Preheat oven at highest available temperature setting, but not higher than 530°F/270°C. If oven offers more than one air-velocity setting, experiment. Use highest velocity that does not blow chaff out of beans, usually low. Until you have established a roasting routine through experiment with your particular oven, set timing function for 25 minutes. Coffee will roast in approximately 12 to 25 minutes, depending on heat-transfer rate of oven and desired degree of roast.

— Spread green beans *close together, one bean deep* (no deeper) across *entire* perforated surface of baking pan. Pour beans onto pan, then pat them down with flattened hand until they are densely but evenly distributed.

— Place baking pan charged with beans in preheated oven.

— Place sample roasted beans where they can be easily seen for color comparison to beans inside oven. Make certain cooling colander and oven mitts are at hand. If you wish to accelerate cooling of beans by water quenching (see pages 169–171), have pump spray bottle ready.

— In about 10 to 15 minutes you should begin to smell coffeelike scent of roasting smoke. If oven is built-in and vents efficiently, you may not smell smoke, and will need to make frequent visual checks of color of roasting beans through oven window until you have established your own timing routine for roasting.

— After appearance of roasting smoke, observe beans through oven window at 1- to 2-minute intervals, making comparison to sample beans. When average color of roasting beans is approximately same as sample, stop oven, pull baking pan out of oven, using oven mitts, and dump beans into colander.

— Over sink or out-of-doors, stir or toss beans in colander until cool enough to touch and until most loose roasting chaff has floated free. To accelerate cooling, water quench as described on pages 169–171. For more on chaff removal, see page 171.

Problems and Refinements

— If you roast same amount of green beans per session and record elapsed time of each session you can begin to predict approximate time your oven requires to achieve a given roast style. Then set kitchen timer for approximately 2 minutes before you anticipate concluding roast. You still must make final decision when to stop roast based on visual observation of bean color, since differences in atmospheric pressure and ambient temperature alter length of a roast from session to session.

— A few convection ovens may roast unevenly (beans at front or back of pan may roast more dark than beans at opposite end, for example). Roasts that are only mildly inconsistent may taste as good as, or better than, more consistent roasts. But if lack of uniformity is extreme or bothers taste, try repositioning roasting pan in a different part of oven, usually toward front or back.

Ovens Combining Conventional and Convection Functions

Some contemporary electric ovens permit cooks to choose options ranging from conventional thermal operation through pure convection to combinations of the two. With such ovens try the combined convection-thermal setting.

Preheat oven to 425°F/220°C to 450°F/230°C. For brighter, more acidy taste in medium roasts and more pungency in dark roasts try upper range of temperature; for more body and less acidity/pungency use lower end of range. Follow instructions given earlier under heading Roasting in a Gas Oven.

Cooling Beans After Roasting

Precise, rapid cooling of freshly roasted beans is essential to good flavor. Home fluid-bed units like the Sivetz modified corn popper and the Sirocco roaster incorporate built-in cooling mechanisms. With other methods you must cool the beans by stirring or tossing them in a colander (*air quenching*) immediately after removing them from the roasting chamber. The cooling process can be accelerated by subjecting the beans to a *light, brief* spray of purified water (*water quenching*) immediately after removing them from the roasting chamber.

Never allow hot beans to sit untouched in a receptacle and cool of their own accord. They will lose considerable aroma and liveliness.

Air quenching beans by stirring or tossing in a colander should be performed over a sink or out-of-doors with stove-top and gas-oven methods, since roasting chaff will be released in the process.

I recommend careful, restrained water quenching for cooling all home-roasted coffee, although for small batches (4 to 6 ounces by weight or volume) simply stirring or tossing the hot beans in a colander is sufficient. If you roast ½ pound or more beans in one session you probably should consider water quenching.

The water-quenching procedure has an added virtue. It reduces the volume of smoke released by the just-roasted beans.

However, it is important that the water quenching be performed *immediately after roasting, sparingly,* and *with care.* No more water must be used than will evaporate almost instantly from the hot beans. Coffee that has been allowed to sit in droplets of moisture during cooling will stale rapidly in the days that follow.

What You Need
— Trigger spray bottle with *adjustable* nozzle.
— Two colanders, large enough to accommodate about twice the volume of green beans you intend to roast.

Procedure
— Fill bottle with distilled or filtered water.
— Adjust nozzle to as *fine* a spray as possible.
— Prepare bottle before beginning roasting and have it and colanders close at hand.
— Apply water *immediately* after dumping beans from roasting chamber into one of two colanders.
— Holding bottle 6 to 10 inches from hot beans, apply a single short (1-second) burst of water to beans while stirring or tossing them in colander. See illustration, page 137.

    Wait a second or two to allow water to evaporate from surface of hot beans, then apply a second short burst and wait another second or two. Repeat intermittent bursts while stirring or tossing beans. *Repeat only as long as water continues to vaporize upon contact with beans.* Normally this will be about one short burst of spray per 1 to 2 ounces of beans.

Do not attempt to completely cool beans with water. Your goal is to *initiate* cooling with a quick application of water, then finish cooling by stirring or tossing. If in doubt stop spraying sooner rather than later.

— Transfer beans, which still will be hot, to second, dry colander. Stir or toss them until they are merely warm. Some moisture may remain beaded on surface of beans immediately after quenching, but if you have performed procedure with restraint this moisture will evaporate well before beans are cool.

Chaff Removal After Roasting

Most green coffee beans are delivered with fragments of the inner skin, or silverskin, of the fruit still adhering to them. During roasting these fragments dry and loosen, turning into roasting chaff.

Decaffeinated beans retain no chaff. Other beans may retain more or less chaff depending on whether they have been subjected to a final cleaning after processing, called polishing.

With hot-air corn-popper and fluid-bed methods the rapid air currents automatically remove chaff from the beans.

With other methods, the recommended cooling procedure—tossing the beans in a colander—will remove most of the loose chaff. Colanders with larger, slotlike openings evacuate chaff more effectively than colanders with smaller circular openings. Occasionally swirling the beans around the inside of the colander with a circular motion will help free the more stubborn chaff fragments.

If you water quench, first quench, then focus on removing the chaff as you toss the beans in the second, dry colander.

Occasionally a coffee will be delivered virtually covered with chaff. In this case pour the beans to and fro between two colanders, tossing and swirling them between pours. Occasionally blow on the beans as you pour them.

Do not become obsessive with this procedure. Eliminate as much loose chaff as you can without making yourself dizzy, then enjoy the coffee.

Resting Coffee After Roasting

Coffee flavor is at its peak 12 to 24 hours after roasting, but don't hesitate to enjoy freshly roasted coffee immediately.

Accommodations for Differences Among Green Coffees

All coffees roast somewhat differently. If you have been roasting one coffee regularly and you begin roasting another, do not expect it to behave exactly like the first.

Any older coffee (past crop, mature, vintage, or aged) tends to roast somewhat faster than a fresh (new crop) coffee. This distinction seldom matters, however, in the hands-on world of home roasting.

More problematic for the home roaster is the delicacy of decaffeinated coffees and the confusing color of aged and monsooned coffees.

Decaffeinated beans roast dramatically (15 to 25 percent) faster than nontreated beans, and must be observed with great care after pyrolysis sets in to avoid overroasting.

A second problem with decaffeinated, aged, and monsooned beans is reading their color during roasting. They begin the roasting process anywhere from light yellow (monsooned beans) to brown (aged and decaffeinated beans). This difference in color means that you must be particularly observant when determining when to end the roast, particularly if you are roasting on the light end of the spectrum.

For advice on compensating for differences among green beans by manipulating temperatures with gas ovens and stove-top corn poppers, see the instructions for those methods earlier in this section.

Roasting Blends of Beans from Different Origins

The various batches of beans from differing origins that together make up most blends can be combined before or after roasting. Blends combined after roasting (after each individual component of the blend has been roasted separately, that is) usually will display more depth and complexity than blends in which all of the components have been roasted together in a single session, since each coffee, when roasted separately, will tend to bring a more fully developed taste profile into the total mix. Furthermore, if you deliberately bring some coffees to a darker or lighter roast, you will add even more complexity to your blend. However, such refinements are time-consuming and may not be worth the effort for most home roasters, who may prefer the simpler approach of blend first, roast later.

The only situation in which two components *must* be roasted separately is in the case of blends of decaffeinated and regular beans, since decaffeinated beans roast much more quickly than untreated beans.

AFTERWORDS

Postroast Flavors and Frills

At this writing producing elaborately flavored coffees with names reminiscent of soda fountains and cocktail lounges—French vanilla, blueberry cheesecake, piña colada, and so on—is the one roasting act you can't pull off at home. These coffees are created with powerful flavoring substances that use a special medium—propylene glycol—to carry the flavor from roasted bean through the brewing process and into the cup. Ordinary kitchen flavorings use water, alcohol, or glycerin as media, all of which fade during brewing. Even the few flavorings available to the home roaster that do make use of propylene glycol are too feeble to persist into the cup. As this book goes to press no supplier of the concentrated professional flavorings is willing to provide them to the home market, presumably for fear that children may find a bottle and overdose on essence of blueberry cheesecake.

If you like extravagant flavors with your home-roasted coffees, add them directly to the cup after brewing, not to the beans before. You can choose from all-purpose extracts and flavorings sold in the spice section of food stores, from the Flavor-Mate brand of unsweetened flavorings packaged in purse- or pocket-sized bottles, from the Italian-style soft-drink syrups used to sweeten and enhance drinks in the espresso cuisine, or from the various powders used to garnish the frothy heads of those drinks. Many of the general books on coffee or espresso listed in Resources (including mine) offer recipes and suggestions for using these flavorings.

What you *can* combine successfully with your freshly roasted coffee beans before brewing are various natural, traditional flavorings. You may want to dress up one of your freshly roasted coffees as a special gift to a friend, for example, or simply experiment with the exotic. If so, here are just a few suggestions for combining traditional ingredients with freshly roasted coffee beans.

Some Prerecipe Caveats

Note that suggested proportions of flavorings to coffee are simply recommended starting points for your own experiments. Spices vary greatly in strength depending on their age and packaging. Furthermore, I generally have gone lightly with flavoring in an attempt to supplement rather than to overwhelm the taste of the coffee. If you prefer dramatic culinary gestures like pesto that can be smelled from the front porch or hot sauces that turn dinner parties into sauna sessions, plan to increase the flavoring proportions from the outset.

My suggestions for pairing specific flavorings and roast styles are even more tentative. The recommended flavorings will enhance any roast style, but the combinations I've noted seem particularly agreeable.

I have avoided specifying powdered spices because one of the advantages of traditionally flavored coffees is the opportunity to grind spice and coffee together. The flavor oils of both are liberated at the same moment, just before brewing.

Choosing Green Coffees for Flavoring

After absorbing the loving descriptions of the world's fine coffees in Chapter 4, readers may wonder about the effect of flavoring on the many subtle taste distinctions I cited and celebrated.

In fact, unless carried out with the greatest discretion, flavorings largely obscure the distinctions among fine coffees. The best coffee for flavoring purposes probably is a good, clean, low-keyed Latin American coffee: a Peru, Mexico, or Brazilian Santos, for example. Indonesian coffees also flavor well. The intense acidity of many East African and high-grown Latin American coffees may compete with some flavors while complementing others.

A Warning on Mills and Grinders

Use only blade-style mills or grinders (the kind that work like blenders and whack the coffee apart) to grind coffees combined with other ingredients. Substances other than coffee can clog or even ruin feed-through, burr-style grinders.

Preparing Dried Citrus Zest

Many of the following recipes depend on the delightful fragrance of the dried outer peel of the orange (the orange zest, as cooks rightly call it). Dried lemon zest also can be attractive in combination with other ingredients.

Suppliers often coat citrus fruits with resins, waxes, or other harmless (yet hardly tasty) substances to preserve freshness. You might want to make a detour to a natural foods store for organically grown, untreated fruits when using the skins to make zest.

To prepare your own zest:

Remove strips of the outer peel of oranges with a paring knife or potato peeler. With oranges feel free to dig into the white inner skin; with lemons use a potato peeler only and try to take as little as possible of the white skin, which will taste bitter.

Place the strips of fresh zest on a cookie sheet in an oven preheated to 200°F/95°C. Remove after 1 ½ hours or when zest is dry and leathery.

Typically 1 orange will produce 6 to 8 strips of zest; 1 lemon 5 to 6 strips.

A few of the spices and dried fruits that can enhance freshly-roasted coffee: star anise; vanilla bean; cinnamon; orange peel; dried, unsugared pineapple.

Orange-Based Coffees

Orange combines particularly well with darker roasts, even the darkest.

Orange-Peel Coffee

For every *fluid* ounce of *roasted* coffee beans:
$1/2$ strip dried orange zest
Break or cut strips into smallish pieces and combine with freshly roasted coffee beans. Prepare for brewing with blade grinder only.
Variations: Partly substitute lemon zest for orange. Or try the zest of bitter Seville oranges.

Vanilla-Orange Coffee

The vanilla both intensifies and softens the orange flavor notes.

For every *fluid* ounce of *roasted* coffee beans:
$1/2$ strip dried orange zest
$1/4$ inch fresh vanilla bean
Break or cut orange strips and vanilla bean into approximately $1/4$-inch pieces and combine with freshly roasted coffee beans. Prepare for brewing with blade grinder only.

Orange-Coriander Coffee

For every *fluid* ounce of *roasted* coffee beans:
$1/2$ strip dried orange zest
$1/4$ teaspoon coriander seeds
Break or cut orange strips into approximately $1/4$-inch pieces and thoroughly combine with coriander seeds and freshly roasted coffee beans. Prepare for brewing with blade grinder only.

Ginger-Orange Coffee

For every *fluid* ounce of *roasted* coffee beans:
$1/2$ strip dried orange zest
$1/8$ to $1/4$ teaspoon chopped dried ginger root
Break or cut orange strips into approximately $1/4$-inch pieces and thoroughly combine with chopped dried ginger and freshly roasted coffee beans. Prepare for brewing with blade grinder only.

Cinnamon-Orange Coffee

This combination produces a superb-flavored coffee. If you try any of these recipes make it this one.

For every *fluid* ounce of *roasted* coffee beans:
$\frac{1}{2}$ strip dried orange zest
$\frac{1}{2}$ inch stick cinnamon
$\frac{1}{4}$ inch fresh vanilla bean
Break or cut orange strips, cinnamon, and vanilla bean into approximately $\frac{1}{4}$-inch pieces and thoroughly combine with freshly roasted coffee beans. Prepare for brewing with blade grinder only.

Cinnamon and Other Spices

Cinnamon alone and nutmeg and cinnamon together are traditional and splendid enhancements to coffee, particularly to light through moderately dark roast styles. Also see earlier recipes combining orange zest and spices.

Anise and various mints similarly resonate well with coffee.

Cinnamon-Stick Coffee

For every *fluid* ounce of *roasted* coffee beans:
1 inch cinnamon stick
Break up cinnamon stick into smallish pieces and thoroughly combine with freshly roasted coffee beans. Prepare for brewing with blade grinder only.

Cinnamon-Vanilla Coffee

The previous recipe allows more coffee taste to emerge; the vanilla in this recipe emphasizes the cinnamon notes.

For every *fluid* ounce of *roasted* coffee beans:
1 inch cinnamon stick
$\frac{1}{4}$ inch vanilla bean
Break or cut cinnamon and vanilla bean into approximately $\frac{1}{4}$-inch pieces and thoroughly combine with freshly roasted coffee beans. Prepare for brewing with blade grinder only.

Cinnamon-Nutmeg Coffee

This coffee is delicious, but take care with the very powerful nutmeg or it will overwhelm everything else.

For every *fluid* ounce of *roasted* coffee beans:
$^3/_4$ inch cinnamon stick
$^1/_{12}$ nut (approximately) nutmeg
$^1/_4$ inch vanilla bean
Lightly crush nutmeg into small crumbs. Break or cut cinnamon stick and vanilla bean into approximately $^1/_4$-inch pieces. Thoroughly combine all ingredients with freshly roasted coffee beans. Prepare for brewing with blade grinder only.

Anise Coffee

The perfume of star anise is a particularly effective enhancement for those moderately dark through dark roasts used for the espresso cuisine.

For every *fluid* ounce of *roasted* coffee beans:
$^1/_2$ (approximately) star-anise cluster
Break up anise clusters into small pieces and thoroughly combine with freshly roasted coffee beans. If anise clusters are already fragmented when purchased, use 2 to 3 pods or star points to every fluid ounce of roasted beans. Prepare for brewing with blade grinder only.

Mint Coffee

I like the gentle taste of spearmint with coffee, but any mint can be used. Some will prefer the brighter, sharper tones of peppermint. Both are particularly pleasant with medium-dark through moderately dark (full-city through espresso) roasts.

For every *fluid* ounce of *roasted* coffee beans:
$^3/_4$ teaspoon dried spearmint
If spearmint is in leaf form, crumble. Thoroughly combine with freshly roasted coffee beans. Prepare for brewing with blade grinder only.
Variation: Substitute $^1/_2$ teaspoon dried peppermint for spearmint, or $^1/_2$ teaspoon of the two combined.

Lemon-Mint Coffee

For every *fluid* ounce of *roasted* coffee beans:
$1/2$ teaspoon dried spearmint
$1/2$ teaspoon lemon grass
$1/4$ strip dried lemon zest

See page 168 for instructions for preparing lemon zest. Cut or tear zest into approximately $1/4$-inch fragments. Combine zest, mint, and lemon grass with freshly roasted coffee beans. Prepare for brewing with blade grinder only.

Vanilla Bean

Vanilla is a magic ingredient when flavoring coffee; in addition to adding its own fragrance it rounds out and intensifies many other flavors, which is why it appears so often in these recipes. Fresh vanilla is another flavor that seems to resonate best with medium-dark through dark (full-city through espresso) roasts.

Vanilla-Scented Coffee

Simply placing vanilla beans and freshly roasted coffee beans together in a sealed container will scent the coffee. Those who take their coffee black may enjoy the sweet, subtle fragrance that results. If you lace your coffee with sugar and milk, however, try the more direct approach embodied in the next recipe.

For every *fluid* ounce of *just-roasted* coffee beans:
$1/2$ inch fresh vanilla bean

Break vanilla bean into $1/2$-inch pieces. Combine with just-roasted coffee beans in a sealed Ziploc bag. Allow to rest for at least 2 days. Before grinding, separate vanilla fragments from coffee beans to be ground and return vanilla fragments to container with remaining beans.

Vanilla-Bean Coffee

For every *fluid* ounce of *roasted* coffee beans:
$1/4$ inch vanilla bean

Cut vanilla bean into $1/4$-inch pieces and combine with freshly roasted coffee beans. Prepare for brewing with blade grinder only.

Chocolate

America's second-most-favorite flavoring after vanilla is best added to the cup following brewing in the form of syrup, extract, or hot chocolate. When added to coffee before brewing, most chocolate is wasted; it fades under the impact of grinding, hot water, and filtering.

However, the following recipe produces a delicately flavored cup that black-coffee drinkers in particular may enjoy. The recipe contains no sugar, but the combination of buttery baking chocolate and fresh vanilla together contribute a smooth, sweet sensation to the cup. The beans also look attractive in their chocolate coating. A medium-dark through moderately dark (full-city through espresso) roast will best accentuate the chocolate tones.

Chocolate-Covered Coffee

For every *fluid* ounce of *green* coffee beans:
¹/₄ square unsweetened baking chocolate
1 inch vanilla bean

Grate chocolate. In warm, moist weather chocolate may require chilling before grating. Place half of grated chocolate into glass, metal, or ceramic bowl. Arrange the following near roasting apparatus: bowl containing chocolate; second, empty bowl; remaining chocolate; and mixing spoon.

Roast coffee. When it reaches desired style, dump directly from roasting chamber into bowl with grated chocolate. Immediately begin stirring hot beans while gradually adding remaining chocolate. Continue stirring until beans are warm and thoroughly coated with chocolate. Dump beans into second, empty bowl and continue to stir until cool. Refrigerate for a few minutes, then remove and break apart any clusters of beans that remain stuck together.

Cut vanilla bean into ¹/₄-inch pieces and lightly mix with chocolate-covered beans. Store in a cool, dry place. Prepare for brewing with blade grinder only.

Orange-Chocolate Coffee

For every *fluid* ounce of *green* coffee beans:
¹/₄ square unsweetened baking chocolate
1 strip dried orange zest (see page 176)
1 inch vanilla bean

Follow preceding recipe for Chocolate-Covered Coffee. Break orange-zest strips into approximately ¼-inch fragments. Combine zest and vanilla-bean pieces with cooled and separated chocolate-covered beans. Prepare for brewing with blade grinder only.

Dried Fruit

Any fruit sufficiently dry to fragment in a grinder can be combined with roasted coffee beans and successfully brewed. Most fruit simply makes the cup heavier and sweeter, however, without adding recognizable flavor notes.

Note that *fruit must be thoroughly dry but not completely brittle.* Think of the consistency of old shoe leather. Most dried fruit sold in markets is too soft; rather than pulverizing, it converts to a sticky mess inside the grinder. Natural-food stores often sell dried fruits that have no sugar added, however, and are stiff to the touch. You may want to experiment by combining some of these fruits with freshly roasted beans. Here is one possibility.

Pineapple-Sweetened Coffee

Look for thinly sliced, unsugared pineapple rounds dried to a leathery consistency. In addition to sweetness and considerable body, they add a muted but recognizable pineapple taste to the cup.

For every *fluid* ounce of *roasted* coffee:
½ thoroughly dried, unsugared pineapple round
Cut or tear pineapple rounds into smallish fragments and combine with freshly roasted coffee beans. When brewing use half again as much of the pineapple-coffee mix as you would unenhanced coffee. Prepare for brewing with blade grinder only.

Storing and Handling Roasted Coffee

Since the primary reason for roasting at home is experiencing the perfume of truly fresh coffee, you obviously should store and handle your roasted coffee with care. Coffee in its green state keeps very well, but the moment it is roasted it begins a rapid, relentless journey from flavorful to flavorless. The taste components of roasted coffee—the elements that make the difference between sour brown water and aromatic pleasure—compose a tiny part of the roasted bean. The enemies of these perfumes are moisture and heat, which destroy them, and oxygen, which stales them. Roasted coffee can be protected from moisture and heat easily enough by storing it in a cool, dry place, out of the sun. But what about oxygen?

The flavor oils are temporarily protected by two elements of the bean: by its physical structure and by the carbon dioxide gas produced as a by-product of roasting.

If you wait to grind your coffee until just before brewing, the physical structure of the bean will do its part. The carbon dioxide is another matter. It steadily filters out of the bean at first, then gradually diminishes in flow as the chemical changes associated with roasting conclude and the roasted bean restabilizes. Meanwhile the ubiquitous oxygen waits, pressing in with vulturelike persistence, waiting its moment to seep into the bean and begin its destruction of the delicate oils.

Coffee tastes best a few hours to a day out of the roaster. By two days after roasting, a good part of the aroma has fallen prey to the opportunistic oxygen; a week later taste is also compromised; in two weeks aroma has virtually vanished and taste has lost its complexity and authority.

Here are some steps to take to preserve and maximize the fragrance of your home-roasted coffee.

Roast small quantities of coffee often. Obviously the best way to drink absolutely fresh coffee is to roast every three to four days.

Store coffee in a cool, dry place, away from direct sunlight. After allowing the coffee to rest for a day uncovered, place in a sealed jar or canister. A canister with a rubber seal and metal clamp is probably best. Caution: *Do not fill a tight-sealing canister or jar more than half-way with just-roasted coffee that has not been rested for a day or so.* The gas escaping from absolutely fresh coffee can exert considerable pressure on the walls and lid of a filled and tightly-sealed container.

Grind your coffee immediately before brewing. The purpose of grinding coffee is to break open the bean and make the flavor oils available to hot water and thus to our palates. Unfortunately, breaking open the bean also makes the flavor oils available to oxygen and staling. Grinding is a devastating procedure that should be undertaken only a few moments before you brew.

Resist the refrigerator reflex. Don't store coffee in refrigerators; they're damp inside, and dampness compromises aroma and flavor. Refrigerators also harbor a variety of odors that can taint freshly roasted beans. Refrigeration seems to mute the flavor even of coffee stored in tightly sealed containers.

Freeze coffee that you can't consume within a few days after roasting. Whether or not it's a good idea to freeze whole-bean coffee is one of those peculiar controversies that run unresolved through the rhetoric of the coffee world. Two of the country's leading technical experts on coffee roasting are diametrically opposed on this issue, one touting the freezer as the perfect place to preserve roasted whole-bean coffee and the other excoriating freezers as the best way to destroy the structural integrity of the bean and its capacity to protect flavor.

I would argue that freezing whole coffee beans is silly while they're fresh, but if you absolutely have to keep your roasted beans around for more than three or four days before brewing, I find the freezer helps considerably more than it hurts. Put the beans in a sound Ziploc freezer bag and squeeze as much air as possible out of the bag before sealing. Remove only as many beans as you intend to consume for the day and immediately reseal the bag and return it to the freezer. Allow the beans to thaw before grinding and brewing.

Drink your coffee immediately after brewing. It does little good to roast, then grind, and brew superbly fresh coffee if you let it sit on a hot plate for ten minutes while the aromatics evaporate. If you must keep brewed coffee around before you drink it, hold it in a preheated thermos, which will preserve the taste if not the aroma.

All of these rules and instructions can be taken either as symptoms of a pointless obsessiveness or, if you love coffee, as a way of being, of stopping to savor a small but exquisite space in the onrush of life.

For more information on coffee brewing, see my books *Coffee: A Guide to Buying, Brewing & Enjoying* and *Espresso: Ultimate Coffee.*

Cupping Coffee at Home

Obviously the most reliable long-term way to evaluate coffee is to drink it the way you usually drink it, but mindfully. But if you're after a knowledge of coffee in its larger complexity and variety, you may want to approach tasting more systematically.

The professional cupping ritual has a relatively long history. It appears to have been well established in its present form by the mid-nineteenth century. Variations of it are used today by coffee growers, agricultural boards and graders, exporters and importers, and roasters and blenders as a way of evaluating coffee and what we do to it.

Traditional cupping is redolent of a sort of mahogany-toned, nineteenth-century romance. The gestures are arcane yet functional, and the trappings—sample roasters, water kettles, silver spoons, and spittoons—as solid yet mythic as the fittings of an old ship or country store.

Although turning a part of your house into a permanent cupping facility is not a practical alternative even for fanatics, a simple, portable adaptation of the professional cupping ritual is. Home cupping provides an effective way to compare similar coffees roasted to different styles, different coffees roasted to the same style, and your own blending experiments.

Setting Up for Cupping

Before cupping you might review the tasting terms defined on pages 58–61, and the reference guide to roast styles on pages 68–69.

You will need identical or almost identical cups or heatproof glasses, one for each coffee, roast, or blend you plan to taste, and a round metal soup spoon. Cups or glasses that flare out a bit at the top are best.

The professional coffee-cupping ritual, taken from a 1920s photograph. Nothing much has changed today except the hats and the gender of some of the cuppers. Coffee growers, exporters, buyers, and roasters regularly cup coffees for purposes of evaluation. Samples of green beans are prepared in small roasters like those pictured on page 64 and in the background here, uniformly ground, and brewed in identical cups. The tasters sample the aroma of each coffee, then repeatedly taste the coffee by sucking it explosively from round spoons, spraying it across their palates. The tasted mouthfuls are finally deposited in the large spittoon in the foreground.

Ideally you also need a burr grinder, one that has settings from fine to coarse, so you can be certain that you are grinding each sample exactly like the others. However, since burr grinders are relatively expensive ($50 and up) you may end up using a blade grinder, one that whacks the coffee apart like a blender. If you do use a blade grinder make sure to time yourself, so that you produce an approximately similar grind for each sample coffee.

You also should have two glasses of water, one to sip from to clear your palate and one in which to rinse the spoon between samples. Finally, you will need a bowl or large mug in which to dispose of mouthfuls of coffee and floating grounds scooped off the surface of the brewed coffee.

Have paper and pencil at hand to take notes. You may find the sample tasting charts reproduced at the end of this section useful.

If you are comparing several green coffees at one sitting, you probably should roast your samples using the recommended design of hot-air corn popper or a similar small fluid-bed roaster, even though you normally employ another method. Consistency of roast style and color over a range of small samples is relatively easy to achieve with hot-air poppers; simply roast the same volume of each sample to the same color (or better yet, to the same bean temperature if you are using a candy thermometer as heat probe) and cool each in the identical way. Roast all of the samples for a given cupping session on the same day.

Cupping Procedure

Grind small samples of each of the coffees you plan to cup. The grind or degree of granulation should be as uniform as possible from one sample to the next. About a medium grind is best. Without becoming obsessive about it, try not to mix coffees from your various samples while grinding. Sometimes coffee will cake up in various spots in a grinder receptacle. In this case, try to knock out the caked portions of one sample before grinding the next.

Place the same volume of ground coffee in each cup or glass. Use about two level tablespoons or one standard coffee measure per six-ounce cup. Meticulous professional cuppers weigh out $1/4$ ounce (seven grams) of coffee per five ounces (150 milliliters) of hot water. Such precision is not important in general cupping, but consistency among samples is.

When all of your samples are prepared, fill each cup with an identical volume of water heated to brewing temperature (a little short of boiling). As you pour the water over the coffee make certain you wet all of the grounds. Fill the cups to about a half-inch below the lip.

Allow the coffee to brew for about three minutes before beginning the cupping.

The cupping itself is in three parts.

Breaking the crust and sampling the aroma. A layer of saturated grounds will cover the surface of the coffee. Bend over the cup with your nose almost touching the coffee, and gently break this crust with your spoon. As you do so, *sniff*. Sniff deeply and repeatedly, while lightly agitating the surface of the coffee with your spoon. Make mental and perhaps written note of the characteristics and intensity of the aroma of each sample. Be active; move back and forth between samples, breaking the surface of each coffee again to refresh the aroma.

Tasting the coffees hot. Breaking the crust and agitating the surface usually provide sufficient activity to sink most of the grounds floating on the surface of the coffee to the bottom of the cup. However, you may need to remove some of the more stubbornly buoyant fragments of ground coffee with your spoon before tasting, particularly if you used a blade grinder.

The professional cupper lifts a spoonful of the coffee and, in a quick, explosive slurp, sprays the coffee across the entire range of membrane in the oral cavity. This is not an easy act to master, particularly given the training most of us receive in how to behave at table. Nevertheless, give it a try. The idea is to get a quick, comprehensive jolt of simultaneous taste and aroma. Note acidity, nuances of acidity, and taste; if the roast is a dark one note the balance of pungent, sweet, and acidy notes. *Don't swallow the coffee.* Instead, roll it around in your mouth, chew it, wiggle your tongue in it. Get a sense of its weight or body, and the depth and complexity of its flavor. Observe how the various sensations develop as the coffee remains in your mouth; some coffees may grow in power and resonance while others may peak and fade.

Now once again you need to defy table manners and spit out the coffee. Professional cuppers use three-foot-high spittoons for this purpose. Obviously you don't need a spittoon; a bowl or mug will do.

Taste repeatedly. Rinse the spoon between samples, and occasionally take a sip of water to clear your palate. Record your observations before moving on to the final part of the cupping.

Tasting the coffees lukewarm. Certain characteristics emerge most clearly at lukewarm or even room temperatures. Let the coffees sit for a few minutes, then return to repeat the cupping, refining and confirming your earlier observations.

Cupping Experiments

You can amuse yourself plus establish some general sensory reference points for cupping by conducting a few simple exercises.

Cupping roast styles. I give rather elaborate instructions for experimenting with roast styles on pages 140–145. Essentially, you roast the same green coffee to four or five progressively darker styles, then line them up and taste them. This gives you some genuine experience to attach to the generalizations about the changing taste profiles of roast styles given in the reference guide on pages 68–69.

Cupping unblended or varietal coffees. Here the emphasis is on the taste characteristics the green coffee brings to the roast, rather than visa versa. Consequently, bring a variety of green coffees to the same, light-to-medium roast (often called a cupping roast). As a palate-training exercise, I suggest you start with very different green coffees, one from each of the general categories proposed in the blending lists on pages 98–99. For example, a Sumatra, a Kenya, a Brazilian Santos, and one of the cited Costa Rican coffees. Taste for the full body and low-toned, rich acidity of the Sumatra, the full body and high-toned, powerful, winelike acidity of the Kenya, the softer profile and lighter body and acidity of the Santos, and finally the full body and clean, classic taste and robust acidity of the Costa Rica.

Then perhaps explore within each flavor family. Cup a Yemen Mocha, an Ethiopian Harar, a Zimbabwe, and a Kenya, for example. Learn to distinguish the lighter body of the Harar, the wild notes of the Mocha and Harar, the heavier body of the Kenya, and the subtle differences among the high-toned, winy acidity they share.

Cupping your own blends. Obviously the idea here is to evaluate your blending experiments. Either maintain the same blend constituents and cup a variety of proportions among them, or keep the proportions the same and cup a series of blends that vary one of the constituent coffees.

Cupping straight coffees and blends roasted for the espresso cuisine. The only way to properly evaluate coffee designed for espresso is to taste it as espresso. I suggest you first prepare identical one-ounce samples (short pulls), using your espresso machine, taste them without sugar or frothed milk, then prepare another series of samples and taste them the way you normally drink your espresso. For detailed information on espresso brewing and cuisine, see my book *Espresso: Ultimate Coffee.*

Sample Tasting Charts

Use the first chart for cuppings in which your goal is to distinguish among green coffees or blends of green coffees. Use the second to compare roast styles, the way in which a given coffee or blend responds to different degrees or styles of roast, and so on. Also use the second chart to compare coffees and blends brought to dark-roast styles. The first three terms—*aroma, acidity,* and *body*—represent key traditional coffee-tasting categories. The categories that follow are less fixed by tradition and usage. Everyone who cups coffee has favorite terms and categories; these last are mine. See pages 58–61 for definitions.

Tasting Chart for Comparing Green Coffees and Light- to Medium-Roast Blends

Name of coffee, mark or estate, grade, crop or age; description of blend:

Date of Cupping:

Tasting Category	Rating*	Notes
Aroma		
Body		
Acidity		
Complexity		
Depth		
Varietal distinction		
Sweetness		
Balance		

* 5 = Extraordinary; 4 = Outstanding; 3 = Satisfactory; 2 = Weak; 1 = Negligible

Tasting Chart for Comparing Differing Roast Styles or Coffees Brought to Dark Roasts

Name of coffee, mark or estate, grade, crop or age; description of blend:

Approximate roast style and other roast notes:

Date of Cupping:

Tasting Category	Rating*	Notes
Aroma		
Body		
Acidity		
Complexity		
Depth		
Varietal distinction		
Sweetness		
Pungency		
Balance		

* 5 = Extraordinary; 4 = Outstanding; 3 = Satisfactory; 2 = Weak; 1 = Negligible

Resources

As home roasting grows in popularity, more sources for equipment and green coffee doubtless will develop. As it is now, supplying home roasting may feel more like a scavenger hunt than shopping. Independent types may glory in the challenge; others will become impatient. I hope that the following information helps.

All-Purpose Mail Order Sources

Some mail-order sources specialize in supporting home roasting across the board, from roasting paraphernalia to green beans. These include the excellent Roast Your Own Coffee Company on the West Coast; Island Coffee, Tea and Spice on the East Coast; and Home Roaster Coffee and Supply Company in the Midwest. For contact information for these and all suppliers listed in this section, see pages 205–208.

Buying Green Coffee Locally

Stores that roast their coffee on the premises or nearby usually will sell you green coffee, particularly if you are willing to buy five or ten pounds at a time. You should pay about 15 to 25 percent less than the roasted price, although some stores will insist on charging the same price for both green and roasted.

Selling unroasted coffee is a fussy inconvenience for most stores because it constitutes an exception to their normal routine. You may not be offered much choice in the way of exotic or out-of-the-way coffees unless you establish a special relationship with the proprietor or manager. Also, be prepared to tolerate arrogant or uncomprehending store clerks. ("What? *You* roast coffee?")

Buying Green Coffee Through the Mails

Consequently you may be forced to pursue an interest in unusual coffees via the mails.

A surprising number of smaller mail-order roasters will sell you five pounds of any coffee they carry green. Just ask. And again, expect about a 15 to 25 percent discount from the by-the-pound roasted price.

Some mail-order companies either specialize in selling small amounts of green coffee to home roasters or invite small green-coffee orders. Here are a few. For contact information, see pages 205–208.

> Armeno Coffee Roasters, Northborough, Massachusetts
> > (Sells any coffee in stock green at a standard reduction from the roasted price; one-pound minimum.)
> The Coffee Critic, South San Francisco, California
> > (Large selection; one-pound minimum.)
> Fante's, Philadelphia, Pennsylvania
> > (One-pound minimum for four basic green coffees in stock; will supply virtually any green coffee available on the U.S. market in one week at a minimum order of ten pounds.)
> Home Roaster Coffee and Supply, Edina, Minnesota
> > (Large selection; one-pound minimum.)
> Island Coffee, Tea and Spice, Flushing, New York
> > (Mail-order house dedicated to the home roaster; large selection; will match any documented per-pound price for a given green coffee; one-pound minimum.)
> Palani Plantation, Palo Alto, California
> > (Small selection; one-pound minimum.)
> Roastery Development Group, New Orleans, Louisiana
> > (Large selection; five-pound minimum.)
> Sivetz Coffee, Inc., Corvallis, Oregon
> > (Small selection; eight-pound minimum.)

Green Coffee in Bulk

By "in bulk" I mean seriously in bulk: a full-sized, 100- to 150-pound bag. Such a purchase can net impressive savings per pound, but requires special arrangements with either a large roaster or a green-coffee dealer. If you can find a local source and pick up the coffee yourself, you will save shipping charges, which can add considerably to the coffee's cost.

An approach that has the potential of netting even more savings is buying a full bag directly from a wholesale green-coffee dealer. At one time these firms were concentrated in large port cities, but since the advent of faxes and E-mail their offices have been dispersing all over the country. If you live in a large metropolitan area you might check the heading "Coffee—Brokers" in the yellow pages. (In some cities this heading may appear only in a separate business-to-business version of the yellow pages. Brokers as a blanket term for all green-coffee wholesalers is a misnomer, by the way. True coffee brokers are usually middlepeople who arrange for green-coffee sales but never take possession of the coffee. Green-coffee dealers actually purchase the coffee and store it in their own warehouses. Obviously, you are looking for a green-coffee dealer rather than a broker, despite the partiality of the telephone companies for the latter term.)

At any rate, call the numbers you find under the broker heading and ask the respondents if they sell single bags. A few will do so happily; many won't even think about it. Some—those who are true coffee brokers rather than dealers—may deal only in enormous containers of coffee. If you do find a source you should pay about one-third (certainly no more than one-half) of the typical roasted price for that coffee.

Here are just a few green coffee dealers who I know for certain will sell and arrange shipping for a single bag. Three of the listed dealers also either sell in quantities even less than a single bag or will split bags, meaning that for a flat split fee added to the per-pound price of the coffee they will repackage and ship a portion of a 100- to 150-pound bag. *Most wholesale dealers do not split bags*, however, and the occasional dealer who does should not be asked to ship less than fifty pounds. If you want really small amounts of a green coffee, see the suppliers listed on page 194.

> Coffee Source, Miami, Florida
> > (25- and 50-pound packages of Costa Rican and Panama
> > Boquete coffee shipped directly from Costa Rica.)
> Dallis Brothers, Inc., Ozone Park, New York
> > (Will split bags for a $5 fee.)
> Interamerican Commodities, Houston, Texas
> Josuma Coffee Company, Menlo Park, California
> > (Handles Indian coffees only.)

Knutsen Coffees, Ltd., San Francisco, California
M.P. Mountanos, Inc., South San Francisco, California
Roastery Development Group, New Orleans, Louisiana
      (Will split bags.)
Royal Coffee, Inc., Emeryville, California
      (Organic as well as conventionally grown coffees.)
Sustainable Harvest Coffee Co., Emeryville, California
      (Specializes in organic and sustainably grown coffees.)

Burlap Bags for Coffee Storage

Those who wish to support their roasting hobby seriously by
establishing a cellar of green coffees will need something suitable in
which to store medium-sized quantities of those coffees. The burlap
"sand" bags used to control flooding are technically sound, hold
about 20 to 25 pounds of green coffee when filled, look suitably professional, come with a simple string closure, and currently cost less
than a dollar per bag.

Look in your yellow pages under a heading that has "Bags" in the
title. In my area the heading is reassuringly specific: "Bags—Burlap
& Cotton." Names of several concerns in obscure industrial parts of
town should follow. Make sure you buy the burlap and not the plastic
bags. Some bag suppliers may have additional styles of small burlap
and cotton bags available as well.

Home Fluid-Bed Roasters

The Sivetz home roaster (see pages 127–129 and 158–161;
$185) and modified heat guns ($100 and $165) only can be pur-
chased by mail from Michael Sivetz. At this writing odd-voltage versions of the excellent Sirocco roaster (pages 127–129 and 158–161)
are available at a hefty price from Armeno Coffee Roasters, which
also stocks paper filters and replacement glass roasting chambers for
the Sirocco. For information on the MacCochran coffee-roasting
adapter (see page 42), call MacCochran Coffee. For information on
the new fluid-bed roaster due out in 1997 and based on the Harold
Gell/Brian Porto patents (pages 41–42), call Armeno Coffee Roasters
or The Coffee Critic. For availability of still another home fluid-bed
roaster attempting to move from prototype to sales, the Unisar Arōsta,
call Unisar. Again, contact information for all listed vendors appears
on pages 205–208.

Improvised Equipment

Theater II Corn Popper. This device (around $25) is usually available in any well-stocked cookware or department store. If not, order from Wabash Valley Farms.

Hot-Air Corn Poppers. Use only the recommended-design popper (see page154) for coffee roasting. Currently two very widely distributed brands incorporate the proper coffee-friendly design; you should be able to turn one up in most regular or discount department stores at $15 to $25. If you find more than one brand incorporating the recommended design, buy the model with the higher wattage indicated on the bottom.

Candy/Deep-Fry Thermometers. Inexpensive metal-stemmed thermometers designed for candy making or deep frying are widely sold in kitchenware departments and stores. Those manufactured by Cooper, Springfield, and Taylor are all about the right length to monitor either air temperature (with the Theater II popper) or internal bean temperature (with recommended designs of hot-air poppers).

Most candy/deep-fry thermometers for sale in consumer outlets are calibrated only to 400°F/200°C, too low (it would seem) for coffee-roasting applications. However, you should have no trouble approximating readings to 500°F/260°C or higher. See page 152.

Universal Enterprises (UEI) imports a thermometer calibrated to 550°F/290°C (Model T550). Its shaft is a bit too short for use in monitoring internal bean temperatures in recommended designs of hot-air poppers, but it can be used successfully to register air temperature in the Theater II stove-top popper. You may have to search to find one. Call Universal Enterprises for availability in your area, or inquire at restaurant supply stores listed in your yellow pages. However, don't be concerned if you are limited to one of the 400°F/200°C models.

Oven Roasting Pans and Supplies. Both the Palani Plantation oven-roasting kit (an aluminum foil pan and a half-pound of green beans) and single roasting pans are available directly from Palani Plantation at very reasonable prices. Contact Palani for a current catalog and price list.

The Palani foil pans are reasonably durable, but eventually break down. General-use perforated oven pans with the right size and pattern of perforations work almost as well and are considerably more durable. At this writing the best are distributed by Mirro/Crispi Crust:

> Crispi Crust Perforated Baking Pan, item #825; under $15.
> Crispi Crust AirBake Perforated Pizza Pans; various prices depending on size, seldom over $15.

All may be difficult to find. Call Mirro/Crispi Crust for retail availability in your area or order directly from Cook's Corner.

Convection Ovens. These appliances produce a coffee that may taste pleasantly mild to some, bland and without aroma to others. See pages 166–169. If possible roast coffee in someone else's convection oven and taste it before buying a convection device purely for that purpose.

Convection ovens are sold in most large appliance and department stores. They can cost as little as $70 to as much as $250. The Aroma AeroMatic Glass Pot Model AST-850 is a good unit for coffee roasting; call Aroma Manufacturing for availability in your area.

Professional Equipment

Sample roasters. Small sample roasters of the traditional drum design roast from four ounces to a pound or more of coffee and are a logical choice for the aficionado sufficiently committed to spend $3,000 to $4,000 for an appliance that is wonderfully picturesque and essentially indestructible.

Jabez Burns (now a division of Buffalo Technologies Corporation) and Probat are the traditional providers of sample roasters to the American coffee trade. The Burns 1X one-cylinder model is available in gas, propane, or 220-volt electric versions at $3,600 to $4,000. It roasts from four to twenty ounces per batch. Probat's elegant PRE-1 sample roaster is available only in a 110-volt electric version, roasts four ounces of coffee per batch, and costs around $4,200. Both are available through Roastery Development Group or directly from Buffalo Technologies or Probat.

The San Francisco SF1-LB sample roaster is essentially a tiny replica drum roaster with most of the features and all of the charm of the larger shop machines. It roasts from four ounces to one pound per batch and is currently available from Coffee/PER in a gas version for $3,500 and a 220-volt electric model at $4,000.

Small shop roasters.   These machines are sometimes divided into two categories: tabletop or micro-roasters (extremely compact machines that turn out three to six pounds per batch) and somewhat larger (and larger-capacity) shop roasters. Prices start at around $7,000 and range up to $16,000 or more, making these units unlikely choices for the coffee hobbyist. Still, who am I, a mere Volkswagen owner, to make assumptions about how much discretionary income others are willing to expend on a culinary obsession?

The marginally least expensive and probably most compact small shop roasters are manufactured and sold by Rair Systems. The Rair roasters are essentially powerful commercial-strength convection ovens that incorporate a perforated roasting drum. At this writing Rair roasters start at about $7,000.

Roasting pioneer Michael Sivetz's current line of six fluid-bed roasters starts with a five-pound-per-batch model at around $7,000. The Australian Roller Roaster (distributed in the United States by Majestic Coffee & Tea) is a well-engineered and very compact fluid-bed tabletop roaster, but its sophisticated electronic monitoring and control apparatus drive its price into the $15,000-plus range. The larger and flashier but similarly electronically gifted Louisville Roaster costs about the same.

The various sample roasters noted earlier should more than satisfy the needs of serious hobbyists who crave the romance and hands-on control of a classic drum roaster, but excellent larger and considerably more expensive equipment is available from several manufacturers. Small drum roasters in the $7,000-to-$10,000 range are produced by Petroncini and Sasa/Samiac, Italian and French manufacturers respectively, both carried by several distributors, including Roastery Development Group. Somewhat larger equipment currently available includes the San Franciscan roaster from Coffee/PER, the Diedrich roasters with their infrared technology, the Probat line of roasters, the Italian Vittoria line, as well as shop-sized and larger roasters from Petroncini and Sasa/Samiac.

Professional Cupping Equipment

A good comprehensive source for classic cupping-room supplies, apparatus, and furnishings (cups, spoons, spittoons, scales, and so on) is the Roastery Development Group.

Flavorings

Professional-strength unsweetened flavorings. These are the flavorings used by professional roasters to create coffees ranging from the now-classic hazelnut-vanilla to outlandish concoctions like banana split or kiwi-mango.

At this writing I have been unable to convince anyone in the flavor-vending network to sell these potent flavorings in small batches for the home market. The situation may change. Consult the home-roasting newsletter *Chaff* or contact me (see page 208).

Traditional flavorings. For whole spices, unsweetened dried fruit, and similar traditional flavorings, try large natural-foods stores or upscale supermarkets.

Further Information

You are holding in your hand the only currently available book-length print source for information on home roasting. A video tape (*Roast Your Own: Your Guide to Coffee Roasting*) that covers mainly pan roasting is available from Island Coffee, Tea and Spice. *Chaff, The Home Roasters Newsletter,* is an informal but invaluable source for the home roaster. If you are computer-enabled you can browse the World Wide Web sites listed on page 203 as well as coffee-related news groups for information on home roasting.

General books on coffee often include valuable information on roasting, although I have synthesized most of the currently available print material in the preceding pages. Seminars on tasting and roasting are useful, but typically expensive, and aimed at novice professionals rather than hobbyists.

The home roaster may find the following sources most useful for information on aspects of coffee other than roasting itself: green-coffee selection, brewing, coffee recipes, and the like.

Books. Espresso Man Books supplies most of the books mentioned below through the mails. Call for the excellent Espresso Man catalog. In addition to its own very useful publications, the Specialty Coffee Association of America may be expanding its book inventory to include many of the titles listed here.

<u>General:</u> My own *Coffee: A Guide to Buying, Brewing & Enjoying* (4th edition) probably provides the most detailed general overview of specialty-coffee matters. Charles and Violet Schafer's *Coffee* is also

excellent, as are Corby Kummer's *The Joy of Coffee*, Timothy Castle's *Perfect Cup: A Coffee Lover's Guide to Buying, Brewing, and Tasting*, and *The Book of Coffee and Tea* by Joel, David, and Karl Schapira. All of these books retail for under $15. The somewhat more expensive hardcover *The Coffee Companion* by London-based Jon Thorn is particularly strong on coffee origins. Michael Sivetz's little self-published introduction to the specialty coffee business, *Coffee Quality*, is outspoken, a bit cranky, graphically clumsy, and biased toward fluid-bed roasting technology, yet still contains considerably more genuine coffee insider information than any ten slick little coffee books filled with repetitive recipes and color photography of croissants. It is available only from Sivetz Coffee.

Considerably more expensive (from $50 to $100) and more expansively illustrated overviews start with William Ukers's *All About Coffee* (2nd edition), an obviously dated (1935) but superb compendium with almost biblical stature in the coffee industry. Reprints are available through the Specialty Coffee Association of America Fulfillment Center. Ian Bersten's recent *Coffee Floats, Tea Sinks* includes excellent, thoroughly illustrated chapters on the history and theory of roasting, although Bersten's theoretical conclusions are somewhat limited by his commitment to fluid-bed technology.

Technical books on coffee are useful for the devotee with patience and a good scientific dictionary, but expensive. The comprehensive one-volume technical overview *Coffee: Botany, Biochemistry and Production of Beans and Beverage*, edited by M. N. Clifford and K. C. Willson, is out of print, but you may be able to find a copy at larger libraries. Michael Sivetz's *Coffee Technology*, coauthored with N. W. Desrosier, is extremely useful despite its lean in the direction of fluid-bed roasting. It too is out of print, but photocopied reprints are available from Sivetz Coffee at around $75. Technical overviews currently in print all cost over $100 per volume. They include the five-volume set *Coffee*, edited by R. J. Clarke and Robert Macrae (roasting is covered in Volume 2, *Technology*), and two volumes by Bernhard Rothfos, *Coffee Production* and *Coffee Consumption*.

The *Proceedings* of the annual conferences of the Specialty Coffee Association of America (available from the SCAA) make fascinating browsing for the enthusiast, although most of the material is aimed at the coffee professional or entrepreneur.

History: Most authoritative sources are expensive ($35 to $100). Ukers's *All About Coffee* is essential, as is Bersten's *Coffee Floats, Tea Sinks*. Bersten is particularly strong on the technical history of coffee.

Edward and Joan Bramah's *Coffee Makers: 300 Years of Art and Design* is another excellent, expensive, and profusely illustrated technical history of coffee making, emphasizing the British experience. Ulla Heise's *Coffee and Coffee Houses* focuses on the social and cultural history of coffee. The early story of coffee in the context of Islamic culture is elegantly and authoritatively covered in Ralph Hattox's crossover academic work *Coffee and Coffeehouse: The Origins of a Social Beverage in the Medieval Near East*, available in an inexpensive paperback edition.

Green coffee: The standard (and expensive) reference work is Philippe Jobin's *The Coffees Produced Throughout the World*.

Cupping: The main source for professional cupping terminology and procedure is Ted Lingle's *The Coffee Cupper's Handbook: A Systematic Guide to the Sensory Evaluation of Coffee's Flavor* (shorter version *The Basics of Cupping Coffee*).

Espresso: My *Espresso: Ultimate Coffee* is the most thorough of currently available overviews. Nick Jurich's *Espresso from Bean to Cup* also is excellent. Riccardo and Francesco Illy's considerably more expensive *The Book of Coffee: A Gourmet's Guide* (previous title *From Coffee to Espresso*) is authoritative and impressively illustrated but short on practical kitchen detail.

Consumer newsletters. Again, *Chaff, The Home Roasters Quarterly* is a chatty, informal, and informative source for home-roasting information, published by Robert Piacente, proprietor of Island Coffee, Tea and Spice. *Kevin Sinnott's Coffee Companion* brings you the voice of a charming coffee obsessive interviewing coffee personalities and meticulously reviewing selected pieces of coffee equipment, including occasional roasting apparatus, in a no-advertising format.

Consumer magazines. *Coffee Journal* is an attractive, well-written and -edited quarterly aimed at the aficionado. Seattle-based *Café Olé* (the original, pioneering coffee-culture magazine) and *Fresh Cup* from Portland, Oregon, are consumer monthlies that retain a pleasantly youthful Northwest coffee-culture orientation despite their growth into national magazines.

Industry magazines and newsletters. *Tea and Coffee Trade Journal* is the granddaddy of coffee trade magazines. It attempts to appeal to larger traditional coffee concerns as well as to the exploding specialty segment of the coffee industry, as does *World Coffee &*

Tea (WC&T). Both are being pressed by *Coffee Talk Magazine* and *Specialty Coffee Retailer*, devoted exclusively to the specialty segment. The SCAA's newsletter *In Good Taste* comes with membership in the association.

Agtron/SCAA Roast Classification Color Disk System. Available from the Specialty Coffee Association of America ($240; SCAA members, $140). Intended for small-scale professional roasters, this kit will be of interest only to the most committed and technically obsessive of home roasters. See pages 57–58 and the inside back cover.

Video tapes.   Careful instruction on simple pan roasting is provided by BG Media's *Roast Your Own: Your Guide to Coffee Roasting*, available through Island Coffee, Tea and Spice. *Gourmet Coffee: Your Practical Guide to Selecting, Preparing and Enjoying the World's Most Delicious Coffees* is an entertaining and accurate, though not particularly detailed overview of specialty coffee generally. A Flessing & Flessing and Walters production, it can be obtained through Video Research Institute or Island Coffee, Tea and Spice. *The Art of Coffee* from Bellissimo Media Productions focuses on practical instruction in brewing procedure. All three tapes retail for $20 to $25.

On-line.   Home roasting seems to appeal to the same active, do-it-yourself types who enjoy going on-line. It crops up often on coffee-oriented World Wide Web sites and news groups.

At this writing more than three hundred web sites offer coffee information. Two good places to start are Tim Nemeck's Over the Coffee (http://www.cappuccino.com), which tries to connect you to as many other coffee sites as feasible, and Lucidcafé (http://www.lucid cafe.com/lucidcafe/), a location offering a variety of excellent coffee-related material and activity, including excerpts from my writing. Also check Cybercafe (http://www.bid.com/bid/cybercafe/).

Seminars and classes.   At this writing almost all coffee-related seminars and classes are aimed at those in or entering the specialty coffee business. Probably the widest range of such activities is carried out by the not-for-profit Specialty Coffee Association of America. The for-profit, somewhat more consumer-oriented Coffee Fest also offers instructional activities at its events. Professional seminars on roasting and related matters are offered by Dallis Bros. and Agtron, a manufacturer of coffee laboratory apparatus, and by Probat, Sivetz Coffee, and other producers of roasting equipment. Contact these organizations for further information.

Associations. The International Association of Home Coffee Roasters (see Contact Information) is brand-new, at this writing, so it is difficult to predict the directions its activities will take. The Specialty Coffee Association of America (SCAA) is a dynamic, well-established catalyst for coffee professionals, and associate membership is open to nonprofessionals. Membership is an excellent way to stay abreast of trends and events in the coffee world, but even associate membership may strike most home roasters as too costly. A visit to the annual Conference and Exhibition can be an informative and eye-opening experience, however.

Contact Information

Agtron, Inc.
1095 Spice Island Drive, Suite 100
Sparks, NV 89431
Voice: 702 685-4600
Fax: 702 685-4611

Armeno Coffee Roasters, Ltd.
75 Otis Street
Northborough, MA 01532
Voice: 508 393-2821
Fax: 508 393-2818

Aroma Manufacturing Company of America
675 Palomar Street
Chula Vista, CA 92011
Voice: 619 585-1441

Bellissimo Media Productions
1800 Valley River Drive, Suite 101
Eugene, OR 97401
Voice: 800 655-3955 (orders)
       503 683-5373 (information)
Fax: 503 683-1010

Buffalo Technologies Corp.
P.O. Box 1041
Buffalo, NY 14240
Voice: 716 895-2100
Fax: 716 895-8263

Café Olé Magazine
150 Nickerson Street, Suite 201
Seattle, WA 98109
Voice: 206 217-9773
Fax: 206 217-9651

Chaff, The Home Roasters Quarterly
46–66 Hollis Court Boulevard, Suite 3
Flushing, NY 11358
Voice: 718 357-6315
Fax: 718 357-6315

The Coffee Critic
1361 Lowrie Avenue
South San Francisco, CA 94080
Voice: 800 427-4842
Fax: 415 952-0555

Coffee Fest
Festivals, Inc.
7525 SE 24th Street, Suite 480
Mercer Island, WA 98040
Voice: 800 232 0083

Coffee Journal
119 North Fourth Street, Suite 211
Minneapolis, MN 55401
Voice: 800 783-4903

Coffee Kids
207 Wickenden Street
Providence, RI 02903
Voice: 401 331-9099
Fax: 401 421-3155

Coffee Source
Dept. 2061
P.O. Box 025216
Miami, FL 33102-5216
Voice: 800 473-3624
Fax: 011 506 257-2908

Coffee Talk Magazine
1306 Western Avenue, Suite 406
Seattle, WA 98101
Voice: 206 382-2112
Fax: 206 623-0446

Coffee/PER, Inc.
111 Freeport Circle
Fallon, NV 89406
Voice: 702 423-8857
Fax: 702 423-8859

Cook's Corner
P.O. Box 220
Manitowoc, WI 54221-0220
Voice: 800 236-2433
Fax: 414 684-5524

Cybercafe
(World Wide Web site)
http://www.bid.com/bid/cybercafe/
1311 West Baseline, Suite 1017
Tempe, AZ 85283
Voice: 800 650-0638
Fax: 520 777-0948

Dallis Bros., Inc.
100-30 Atlantic Avenue
Ozone Park, NY 11416
Voice: 718 845-3010
Fax: 718 843-0178

Damm Kaffeeröstsysteme
Höhenstrasse 4
D-67829 Schmittweiler
Germany
Voice: 011 49-675-394-060
Fax: 011 49-675-394-061

Diedrich Coffee Roasters
1625 Baldy Mountain Road
Sandpoint, ID 83864
Voice: 208 263-1276
Fax: 208 265-4584

Espresso Man Books
165 Midway Avenue
Auburn, CA 95603
Voice: 800 207-4026
Fax: 916 885-5952

Fante's
1006 South Ninth Street
Philadelphia, PA 19147
Voice: 800 878-5557
Fax: 215 922-5723

Fresh Cup Magazine
P.O. Box 82817
Portland, OR 97282-0817
Voice: 503 224-8544

Home Roaster Coffee and Supply Co.
4833 Westbrook Lane
Edina, MN 55436
Voice: 612 922-2238
Fax: 612 922-2238
E-mail: java4u@aol.com

Interamerican Commodities
7600 West Tidwell, Suite 111
Houston, TX 77040
Voice: 713 462-2671
Fax: 713 462-3528

International Association of Home Coffee Roasters
4833 Westbrook Lane
Edina, MN 55436
Voice: 612 922-2238
Fax: 612 922-2238

Island Coffee, Tea and Spice
See *Chaff*

Josuma Coffee Company
P.O. Box 1115
Menlo Park, CA 94026
Voice: 415 366-5453
Fax: 415 366-5464

Kevin Sinnott's Coffee Companion
3 South 681 Melcher Avenue
Warrenville, IL 60555
Voice: 708 393-9010
Fax: 708 393-7107

Knutsen Coffees, Ltd.
660 Sacramento Street, Suite 302
San Francisco, CA 94111
Voice: 415 362-4414
Fax: 415 362-8652

Louisville Roaster Company
P.O. Box 1
San Jose, CA 95103-0001
Voice: 408 258-4503
Fax: 800 700-1651

Lucidcafé
(World Wide Web site)
http://www.lucidcafe.com/lucidcafe/

M. P. Mountanos, Inc.
1361 Lowrie Avenue
South San Francisco, CA 94080
Voice: 800 229-1611
Fax: 415 875-4208

MacCochran Coffee
Voice: 800 589-8960

Majestic Coffee & Tea
3870 Charter Park Drive
San Jose, CA 95136
Voice: 408 448-6370
Fax: 408 448-8537

Mirro/Crispi Crust Consumer Center
P.O. Box 1330
Manitowoc, WI 54221-1330
Voice: 800 527-7727

Over the Coffee/Tim Nemeck
(World Wide Web site)
http://www.cappuccino.com
Voice: 319 393-7738
E-mail: tim@gryffin.com
         tim@netins.net

Palani Plantation
430 Nevada Avenue
Palo Alto, CA 94301
Voice: 415 327-5774
Fax: 415 969-2144

Probat, Inc.
4127 Willow Lake Blvd.
Memphis, TN 38118
Voice: 901 363-5331
Fax: 901 794-9697

Rair Systems, Inc.
430 Lake Cook Road, Suite B
Deerfield, IL 60015
Voice: 708 940-8300
Fax: 708 940-8326

Roast Your Own Coffee Company
369 62nd Street
Oakland, CA 94618
Voice: 800 690-6950

Roastery Development Group
(green-coffee orders)
941 Decatur
New Orleans, LA 70116
Voice: 504 586-8989
Fax: 504 586-9924
(World Wide Web site)
http://www.@coffeebiz.com

Roastery Development Group
(professional roasting and cupping equipment)
245 South Railroad Avenue
San Mateo, CA 94401
Voice: 415 343-1333
Fax: 415 343-2111
E-mail: stuff@coffeebiz.com

Royal Coffee, Inc.
5885 Hollis Street
Emeryville, CA 94608
Voice: 800 843-0482
Fax: 510 547-7223

Sivetz Coffee, Inc.
349 S.W. 4th St.
Corvallis, OR 97333
Voice: 503 753-9713
Fax: 503 757-7644

Specialty Coffee Association of America
One World Trade Center, Suite 800
Long Beach, CA 90831
Voice: 310 983-8090
Fax: 310 983-8091
Fulfillment Center
(for ordering reprints of William Ukers's
All About Coffee)
Voice: 800 647-8292
Fax: 800 647-8292

Specialty Coffee Retailer
P.O. Box 720
Wayzata, MI 55391
Voice: 612 473-5088
Fax: 612 473-7068

Sustainable Harvest Coffee Co.
2000 Powell Street, Suite 1200
Emeryville, CA 94608
Voice: 510 654-2735
Fax: 510 655-7887

Tea & Coffee Trade Journal
130 West 42nd Street
New York, NY 10036
Voice: 212 391-2060
Fax: 212 827-0945

Unisar
151 West 19th Street
New York, NY 10011
Voice: 212 989-5219
Fax: 212 691-1318

Universal Enterprises, Inc. (UEI)
5500 S.W. Arctic Drive
Beaverton, OR 97005
Voice: 503 644-8723

Video Research Institute (VRI)
2015 Airpark Court
Auburn, CA 95602
Voice: 800 786-8433
Fax: 916 888-7421

Vittoria
Via A. Vespucci, 22
44044 Cassana (Fe)
Italy
Voice: 39 532-732463
Fax: 39 532-732557

Wabash Valley Farms
Route 1
Box 43
Quarry Road
Monon, IN 47959
Voice: 800 270-2705
Fax: 219 253-8172

World Coffee & Tea (WC&T) Magazine
1801 Rockville Pike, Suite 330
Rockville, MD 20852
Voice: 301 984-7333
Fax: 301 984-7340

To Contact the Author
By mail: Send your query with a stamped, self-
addressed envelope to:
Kenneth Davids
367 Moraga Avenue
Piedmont, CA 94611
By E-mail: kenneth_davids@ccacoak.edu

INDEX

Page numbers in italics denote illustrations.

Kenneth Davids

Kenneth Davids's formal involvement with coffee began in the early 1970s when he opened a coffeehouse in Berkeley, California. His first book, *Coffee: A Guide to Buying, Brewing & Enjoying*, initially appeared in 1975. Since then it has sold more than 200,000 copies in four editions and has cumulatively helped shape the specialty coffee movement in the United States. A British edition under the title *The Coffee Book* was published in 1980. Mr. Davids's book on espresso, *Espresso: Ultimate Coffee*, appeared in 1994 and was nominated for a James Beard Award. He contributes to consumer and industry coffee periodicals, and excerpts from his publications appear on Lucidcafé, a World Wide Web site. In addition to writing on coffee, he has published a novel and translations. He is a longtime member of the Educational and Promotional Materials Committee of the Specialty Coffee Association of America and has cowritten a script for a video on coffee growing on behalf of the association. He teaches writing and history at the California College of Arts and Crafts in Oakland and San Francisco, and he resides in the San Francisco Bay area.